The Rest of God

When is the Rest?

Larry Wilson

ISBN: 978-1-945975-41-7

Unless otherwise noted, scriptures are taken from the KING JAMES VERSION (KJV): KING JAMES VERSION, public domain.

Published by EA Books Publishing a division of
Living Parables of Central Florida, Inc. a 501c3
EABooksPublishing.com

Acknowledgements

To my parents for bringing me up in a Christian environment, to seek the Lord.

To the Lord Jesus and how He has led us to seek out the Truth, even when there is sometimes pain in learning and relearning, being clay in the potters hands.

To all the people that the Lord has lead in my path to challenge or to enrich my faith.

To The Holy Spirit That the Lord sent to us, for without Him we cannot even begin to understand the Word.

To all the saints that have gone on before understanding what God has said, on how to live, thus laying the foundations for us to follow today.

To all those that seek truth and will allow God to strip away the preconceived ideas, it is like striping corn the husk is the preconceived ideas which we have to get rid of to get to the kernels of truth.

Contents

Foreword

From the time God looked down and saw a man named Abraham. He then began to show Abraham the things to come. How God would choose a people for Himself and would give them the Rest in God they would desire. This would only take place when the children of Israel would harken to the Lord's commands. God set forth the instructions for His people to follow. This is the Sabbath in which you are to Rest. And here is the land that I am giving you to rest in.

For thousands of years people have been looking for the Rest of God. Some have entered into His Rest, while the rest of us have fallen short. The Rest of God comes about when we begin to believe what God has spoken and begin to follow His commands.

For the last 2000 years there have been changes taking place, to change the Word of God. The Christians will say that Sunday is the day of the Lord. Stating that (Jesus) rose from the grave and making this the Lord's Day. While the Jews and the God fearing Gentiles (Christians) worship the Lord on the Sabbath.

Reminding you of the fourth commandment, to remember the Sabbath and keep it holy.

Who is it that will enter into the Rest of God? And how will we go about to enter into His Rest. As we learn about God's Rest we will learn how to enter into God's Rest.

To help us learn about God's Rest, when we answer the questions in the back of this book. It will help us better understand what God is saying about His Rest.

The questions follow the book from the beginning to the end.

Introduction

The Rest of God, When is the Rest of God ? Who will participate in the Rest of God? Is there a certain day and time for His Rest? What is the rest?

As we go through this study on the Rest of God the answers will become clear.

What does the Bible say about God's Rest in the beginning?

> *Thus the heavens and the earth were finished, and all the host of them.*
>
> *And on the seventh day God ended His work, which he had made: and he rested on the seventh day from all the work, which He had made.*
>
> *And God blessed the seventh day, and sanctified it: because that He had rested from all his work which God created and made.* (Genesis 2:1-3)

Here we see that God Rested on the seventh day and He sanctified that day, or to say that He set it apart for a certain purpose, which is for His purpose.

Now, we come to Mount Sinai where God gives forth the everlasting covenant, which we call the Ten Commandments, besides these, God gives many other instructions and statutes and judgments. But let us look at the everlasting covenant to see what God says about His Rest. Let us look at the fourth commandment and see what God tells the whole house of Israel to do along with the other people who had come out of Egypt with them.

> *Remember the Sabbath day, to keep it holy.*
>
> *Six days shalt thou labor, and do all thy work:*
>
> *But the seventh day is the Sabbath of the Lord thy God: in it thou shalt not do any work, thou, thy son, nor thy daughter, thy manservant, nor thy maidservant, nor thy cattle, nor thy stranger that is within thy gates:*

For in six days the Lord made heavens and earth, the sea, and all that is in them, and rested the seventh day: wherefore the Lord blessed the Sabbath day, and hallowed it (Exodus 20:8-11).

Here we see that God tells Israel what to do and when to Rest and who should join into His rest. Israel, their servants, their cattle, and the strangers who were in their gates. God tells them why they were to Rest on His day.

Who is to enter into the Rest of God? Is it Israel the nation only or is it also the strangers, who join themselves to Israel? Who are we? Are we one of the descendants of the nation of Israel or are we descendants of one of the nations of the earth, called Gentiles.

Let's look at what Isaiah says:

For the Lord will have mercy on Jacob, and will yet choose Israel, and set them in their own land: and the strangers shall be joined with them, and they shall cleave to the house of Jacob.

And the people shall take them, and bring them to their place: and the House of Israel shall possess them in the land of the Lord for servants and handmaids: and they shall take them captives, whose captives they were; and they shall rule over their oppressors (Isaiah 14:1-2).

Here we find that it is Israel and the strangers that join themselves to Israel.

These are the ones that will enter God's Rest. It is Israel, it is the strangers, and it is those of us that believe, with a faith that is a working faith. James says in 2:14-26 how works and faith go hand in hand. True faith has the works that back up the belief. Otherwise we fall into the same area as the devils, which believe. They believe but have not works that please God.

But wilt thou know, O VAIN MAN, that faith without works is dead? (James 2:20)

Who shall enter into His Rest, those of us who have the faith and believe what God has said? And put into practice the commandments of God into our lives.

The Rest of God

When is the Rest?

Larry Wilson

THE REST OF GOD

What does the book of Hebrews say about God's Rest?

> *Let us therefore fear, lest, a promise being left us of entering into His (God's) Rest, any of you should seem to come short of it.*
>
> *For we who have believed do enter into Rest,*
>
> *For he spake in a certain place of the seventh day on this wise, And God did Rest the seventh day from all his works.*
>
> *If they shall enter into My Rest.*
>
> *There remaineth therefore a Rest to the people of God* (Hebrews 4:1,2,4,9).

In this study of the REST OF GOD, we shall look at as much of the Bible to see just what God is telling His people. First off, who are God's people? In the beginning and also now. Are you one of God's people?

There are ways of telling which god we serve. Is it God or Satan who is the deceiver?

In the beginning, God looks down and saw the man Abram, tells him to get out of his country, unto a land that He would show him. God took this man and changed his name to Abraham saying, he would become a great nation. This account we can read in the book of Genesis.

From Abraham came Isaac and then Jacob, whose name was changed to Israel.

As we read the books of Genesis through Deuteronomy, we find that God took a people from among the nations to be a people unto

Himself. He tells this people that they would be His people and He would be their God. As we study through the Bible from Genesis through Revelation, God has a people that are to be set apart from all of the other nations. God gave His people standards to live by.

In the beginning of time as we know of it, was the WORD. In the beginning was the Word and the Word was God and is God. And He, being God Rested on the seventh day, not only did He Rest but He sanctified His day.

> *In the beginning God created the heavens and the earth* (Genesis 1:1).

> *Thus the heavens and the earth were finished, and all the host of them, and on the seventh day God ended his work which he had made; and he rested on the seventh day from all his work which he had made. And God blessed the seventh day, and sanctified it: because that in it he rested from all his work which God created and mad.* (Genesis 2:1-3).

What is it to sanctify? The dictionary states as follows:

Sanctify:

- to set apart as holy, for some sacred purpose;
- consecrate
- to make productive of spiritual blessing

Sanctified:

- consecrate
- set apart for holy purposes
- purified, made holy

According to this definition of the word sanctified, God set the seventh day apart from all the other days for a reason and according to His purpose.

> *For my thoughts are not your thoughts, neither are your ways my ways, saith the Lord. For as the heavens are*

> *higher than the earth, so are my ways higher than your ways, and my thoughts than your thought.* (Isaiah 55:8, 9).

God is saying that He will do things His way even if it does not make any sense to us. His ways are better than our ways. We have the nerve to say that we should do it this way or that. The reply would be: when you get to be God then you can do it your way, but right now you should do it my way, that's what the Lord is saying.

In Genesis God rested and He set the seventh day apart. Is there more, let's move on?

> *But the seventh day is the Sabbath of the Lord thy God* (Exodus20:10).

> *For in six days the Lord made the heaven and earth, the sea, and all that is in them, and rested the seventh day: wherefore the Lord blessed the seventh day and hallowed it* (Exodus 20:11).

> *But the seventh day is the Sabbath of the Lord thy God:* (Deuteronomy 5:14)

> *Keep the Sabbath day to sanctify it, as the Lord thy God Commanded the.*(Deuteronomy 5:12).

> *but the seventh is the Sabbath of rest, holy to the Lord:* (Exodus 31:15)

So far God has sanctified, blessed, and hallowed the seventh day of the week. It is a day of Rest, holy to the Lord. Let's take a look at these words from the dictionary and there meanings.

Blessed:

- holy, hallowed, worthy of reverence
- favored with supreme happiness
- enjoying heavenly felicity
- bringing comfort or joy

Hallow:

- to make holy
- to consecrate

- to sanctify
- to set apart
- dedicate or devote to the service or worship of God

Holy:

- dedicated to the service of God
- consecrated
- pure; morally and spiritually perfect
- sinless

Holy day

- a day set aside as sacred, as the Sabbath
- to be observed with religious commemorative ceremonies

Rest:

- the act or condition of being quiet or at peace
- freedom from disturbance of mind or spirit, tranquility, security
- sleep; slumber
- cessation of motion, effort, labor, or exertion of any kind
- a place of quiet or repose; a stopping place
- foundation

Profane:

- not sacred or holy
- having to do with the world
- showing disrespect or irrelevance toward God or sacred things
- unholy, blasphemous
- not privileged to participate in the inner mysteries
- to put to an improper use

- to treat something sacred with irreverence, contempt, abuse, debase

As we use these definitions this will better help us understand what the Father is wanting us to know.

From what we have looked at so far, God is saying that the seventh day of the week is the Sabbath, His day. This is His Holy Day that He has made for us to Rest in Him. In Isaiah 58:13 let's see what the Lord says about the Sabbath.

> *IF thou turn away thy foot from the Sabbath, from doing thy pleasure on MY HOLY DAY; and call the Sabbath a delight, the holy of the Lord, honorable; and shalt HONOR HIM, (God), not doing thine own ways, nor finding thine own pleasure, nor speaking thine own words* (Isaiah 58:13).

God is saying to us that this is His special day. We should do things that please Him on His day.

HIS CHOSEN PEOPLE

As we turn to His people, what did He tell His people to do on His Holy Day, the day of the Lord? We need to see, who are His chosen people. And how did they become the chosen.

To start from the promise made to Abraham and then to Isaac and then to Jacob, (whose name was changed to Israel) and to their descendants. He tells this people that they would be a special people to Him.

> *For thou art a holy people unto the Lord thy God: the Lord thy God hath chosen thee to be a special people unto himself, above all the people that are upon the face of the earth* (Deuteronomy 7:6).

> *Ye are the children of the Lord your God: For thou art a holy people unto the Lord thy God, and the Lord hath chosen thee to be a peculiar people unto himself, above all the nations that are upon the earth* (Deuteronomy 14:1, 2).

> *Blessed is the nation whose God is the Lord; and the people whom he hath chosen for his own inheritance* (Psalm 33:12).

> *But I have chosen Jerusalem that my name might be there; and have chosen David to be over my people Israel* (2 Chronicles 6:6).

This shows us that God has chosen a people to Himself, but we can choose God also. When we choose the Lord to be our God and to rule over us, we do what He says and not what we wish.

> *...Ye are witnesses against yourselves that ye have chosen the Lord, to serve him. And they said we are witnesses.*

> *Now therefore put away, said he, the strange god's which are among you, incline <u>your heart unto the Lord God</u> of Israel.*
>
> *The Lord our God will we serve and his voice will we obey* (Joshua 24:22-24).
>
> *And all the people answer together, and said, All that the Lord hath spoken we will do* (Exodus 19:8).
>
> *And when the Jews were gone out of the synagogue, the Gentiles besought that these words might be preached to them the next Sabbath* (Acts.13:42).
>
> *That the Gentiles, should be fellow heirs, and of the same body, and partakers of his promise in Christ by the gospel* (Ephesians 3:6).
>
> *Neither let the son of the stranger that hath joined himself to the Lord* (Isaiah 56:3).
>
> *Also the sons of the stranger, that join themselves to the Lord, to serve him, and to love the name of the Lord, to be his servants, everyone that keepeth the Sabbath from polluting it, and taketh hold of my covenant* (Isaiah 56:6).

Any one of us can become one of God's chosen people by choosing Him to be our God, and following the conditions He set down for us to follow. Also look at Ezekiel 37, who joins up with Judah.

THE CONDITIONS TO BE HIS CHOSEN PEOPLE

Anyone can become one of God's people when we meet the requirements that He sets forth.

> *Now therefore, if ye will obey my voice indeed, and keep my covenant, then ye shall be a peculiar treasure unto me above all people: for all of the earth is mine: And ye shall be unto me a kingdom of priest, and holy nation* (Exodus 19:5-6).

> *One ordinance shall be both for the congregation, and also for the stranger that sojourneth with you, and ordinance for ever in your generations: as ye are, so shall the stranger be before the Lord* (Numbers 15:15).

> *One law and one manner shall be for you and the stranger that sojourneth with you* (Numbers 15:16).

> *Ye shall have one manner of law, as well for the stranger, as for one of your own country: for I am the Lord your God* (Leviticus 24:22).

We need to obey His voice and keep His covenant; this applies for both Israel and the stranger or the nations, which join themselves to God.

God said the same law would be for both.

Now what are the instructions that God has to His people about HIS HOLY DAY, The seventh day, the Sabbath?

> *Remember the Sabbath day, to keep it holy. Six days shalt thou labor, and do all thy work: But the seventh day is the Sabbath of the Lord thy God: in it thou shalt not do*

any work, thou, nor thy son, nor thy daughter, thy manservant, nor thy maidservant, nor thy cattle, nor thy stranger that is within thy gates: for in six days the Lord made the heaven and earth, the sea, and all that in them is and rested the seventh day: wherefore the Lord blessed the Sabbath day and hallowed it (Exodus 20:9-10).

Verily my Sabbaths ye shall keep: for it is a sign between you and me throughout your generations; that ye may know that I am the Lord that doth sanctify you (Exodus 31:13).

God says that the Sabbath is a sign between Him and us.

Ye shall KEEP the Sabbath therefore, for it is HOLY UNTO YOU: every one that defileth it shall surely be put to death (Exodus 31:14).

The Sabbath shall be Holy to us.

Six days may work be done; but the seventh day is the Sabbath rest holy to the Lord: whosoever doeth any work in the Sabbath day, he shall surely be put to death (Exodus 31:15).

We work on the Sabbath we will be put to death.

Wherefore the children of Israel shall keep the Sabbath, to observe the Sabbath throughout their generations for a perpetual covenant (Exodus 31:16).

The Sabbath is a perpetual covenant throughout all generations.

It is a sign between me and the children of Israel forever: For in six days the Lord made heaven and earth, and on the seventh day he rested and was refreshed.

The Sabbath is a sign forever (Exodus 31:17).

...but on the seventh day there shall be to you a holy day, a Sabbath of rest to the Lord: whosoever doeth any work therein shall be put to death (Exodus 35:2).

It shall be a Sabbath of rest unto you, and ye shall afflict your souls, by a statute forever (Leviticus 16:31).

But the seventh day is the Sabbath of rest, an holy convocation; (a meeting together dedicated to the service of God): ye shall do no work therein: it is the Sabbath of the Lord in all your dwellings (Leviticus 23:3).

Keep the Sabbath day to sanctify it, as the Lord thy God hath commanded thee (Deuteronomy 5:12).

What did God tell His people about the seventh day; Sabbath would be to them, To keep holy, holy day, holy unto you, holy to the Lord, rest, sanctify, a sign, holy convocation, keep throughout their generations, perpetual covenant, statue forever, commanded, no work, don't defile.

If God chooses us or we chose God to be our God then this is what His Sabbaths should mean to us.

There are many other conditions to be God's people, but we are looking just at His Rest. Remember what Israel said at Mount Sinai.

So Moses came and called the elders of the people, and set before them all these words which the Lord had commanded him. And all the people answered together and said, All that the Lord has spoken we will do. And Moses brought back the words of the people to the Lord (Exodus 19:7-8).

THE STRANGER

Who is the stranger? The stranger is a person who is not one of God's people.

> *Moreover concerning the stranger, that is not of thy (God's) people Israel, but cometh out of a far country for thy name's sake* (1Kings 8:41).

Let's take a look at what the definition of a Stranger and a Gentile.

STRANGER:

Strong's number: – H1616- foreigner, alien, sojourner

Dictionary:

- outsider
- visitor, guest
- someone outside has or distinct from a particular group, be social professional, national, language.
- the lack of citizenship to a nation, kingdom in which you are living.

GENTILE:

Strong's number: H1471- a foreign nation

Dictionary:

- any people that are not Jewish
- Christian as distinguished from Jewish
- pagan or heathen
- belonging to a people, nation

Thus saith the Lord God; No stranger, uncircumcised in heart, nor uncircumcised in flesh, shall enter into my sanctuary, of any stranger that is among the children of Israel (Ezekiel 44:9).

And in that day there shall be a root of Jesse, which shall stand for ensign of the people; to it will the Gentiles (nations) seek: and his rest shall be glorious (Isaiah 11:10).

Thus saith the Lord God, Behold; I will lift up my hand to the Gentiles, and set up my standard to the people (Isaiah 49:22).

What is this standard that God gives to the Gentiles (nations), the same that He has given to Israel? These are the standards by which His people live, when we serve the God of Israel.

And the remnant of Jacob shall be among the Gentiles (nations), in the midst of many peoples, (Micah 5:8).

Who is the remnant of Jacob (Israel)? Those that keep (do) the commandments of God and have the testimony of Jesus (Revelation 12:17, 14:12).

The stranger is of the nations of the earth and not of the nation of Israel, which are called the Gentiles. As Israel sojourned through the land, the stranger would fear Israel's God or would fear the Jews and became a Jew.

And in every province, and in every city, whithersoever the king's commandment and his decree came, the Jews had joy and gladness. a feast and a good day. And many of the people of the land became Jews; for the fear of the Jews fell upon them (Esther.8:17).

Many of the strangers became Jews or became part of Israel from the fear that God put on them.

There shall no man be able to stand before you: for the LORD your GOD shall lay the fear of you and the dread of you upon all the land that ye tread upon, as he hath said unto you (Deuteronomy 11:25).

This was a condition, which would take place as long as Israel followed the commandments of God. When Israel transgressed from God then the fear would depart from the nations.

Today the stranger is anyone that is outside of the covenant of God, by not following the covenant that God spoke to all of Israel through Moses.

What does God tell the stranger to do about HIS SABBATHS?

> *Thus saith the Lord, Keep ye judgment, and do justice: for my salvation is near to come, and my righteousness to be revealed.*
>
> *Blessed is the man that doeth this, and the son of man that layeth hold on it; that keepeth the Sabbath from polluting it; and keepeth his hand from doing any evil.*
>
> *Neither the son of the stranger, that hath joined himself to the Lord, speak, saying, The Lord hath utterly separated me from his people: neither let the eunuch say, Behold, I am a dry tree.*
>
> *For thus saith the Lord unto the eunuchs that <u>keep my Sabbaths</u> and choose the things that please me, and take hold of my covenant;*
>
> *Even unto them will I give in mine house and within my walls a place and a name better than that of sons and daughters: I will give them an everlasting name that shall not be cut off.*
>
> *Also the sons of the stranger, that join themselves to the Lord, to serve him, and to love the name of the Lord, to be his servants, every one that keepeth the Sabbath from polluting it, and taketh hold of my covenant:*
>
> *Even them will I bring to my holy mountain, and make them joyful in my house of prayer* (Isaiah 56:1-7).
>
> *If thou turn away thy foot from the Sabbath, from doing thy pleasure on my holy day; and call the Sabbath a delight the holy of the Lord, honorable; and shalt honor*

> *him, not doing thine own ways, nor finding thine own pleasure, nor speaking thine own words:*
>
> *Then shalt thou delight thyself in the Lord; and I will cause thee to ride upon the high places of the earth, and feed thee with the heritage of Jacob thy father: for the mouth of the Lord hath spoken it* (Isaiah 58:13-14).

When we, the strangers, (Gentiles nations) take hold of God's holy day, the Sabbath along with Israel (the Jews), Then God says He will make us to ride upon the high places of the earth. The Lord said the Sabbath is a delight and not a burden.

THE HOLY OR THE PROFANE

The Lord said not to pollute His holy day. What is it to pollute something?

It is to make unclean which is clean, to taint with guilt to destroy that which is good. Such as to take pure clean water, for drinking and make it unclean for drinking by putting dirt into it. We take the pure word of God and pollute it by changing God's word to fit our own needs. Thus we profane the name of God.

God hath said to keep holy the things of His holy.

When God spoke to all of Israel and tells them what He required, then the people replied: what the Lord hath said we will do. But what has happen we have all turn our own way and have profane the things of God.

> *All we like have gone astray; we have turned everyone to his own way* (Isaiah 53:6). Sheep Gone from the truth.
>
> *Which have forsaken the right way, and are gone astray, following the way of Balaam the son of Bosor who loved the wages of unrighteousness. We follow the way of unrighteousness* (2 Peter.2:15).
>
> *For we are not as many, which corrupt the word of God* (2 Corinthians 2:17).

We corrupt the word of God.

> *Making the word of God of none effect through your tradition, which ye have delivered: and many such thing ye do* (Mark.7:13).

We have more respect for our traditions than the Word of God.

> *But in vain do they worship me, teaching for the doctrines the commandments of men* (Matthew 15:9).

Thus we make void the word of God.

We teach the commandments of men and not God and change what God has said.

> *They shall therefore keep mine ordinance, lest they bear sin for it, and die therefore, if they profane it; I the Lord do sanctify them* (Leviticus 22:9).

We profane the commandments of God

> *And they shall not profane the holy things of the children of Israel, which they offer unto the Lord* (Leviticus 22:15).

We profane the holy things of God.

> *Neither shall ye profane my holy name; but I will be hallowed among the children of Israel: I am the Lord, which hallow you* (Leviticus 22:32).

We profane the name of God.

> *Thou hast made void the covenant of thy servant: thou hast profaned his crown by casting it to the ground* (Psalm 89:39).

We make void the covenant.

> *Thou hast despised mine holy things, and hast profaned my Sabbaths* (Ezekiel 22:8).

> *Moreover this they have done unto me; they have defiled my sanctuary in the same day, and have profaned my Sabbaths* (Ezekiel 22:38).

> *...did not your fathers thus, and did not our God bring all this evil upon us, and upon this city? yet ye bring more wrath upon Israel by profaning the Sabbath* (Nehemiah 13:18).

We profane the Sabbath.

To profane the Sabbath, is to bring disgrace on the holy name of God and things of God. The Bible says to be doers of the word and not hearers only, even when it does not make any sense to us. When we walk in the ways of the Lord then He will put His hedge around us. But when we walk after our own ways and man's traditions, then we walk out from under His mighty hand. So the Devil as a roaring lion will seek us out. He can do this by using the word of God to deceive us into comfort and false peace.

The Lord God is looking for men and women to stand in the gap and teach the different between the holy and the profane. But what happens is different.

> *Her priest have violated my law, and have profaned mine holy things: they have put no difference between the holy and profane, neither have they showed difference between the unclean and clean, and have hid their eyes from my Sabbaths, and I am profaned among them.*
>
> *Her princes in the midst thereof are like wolves ravening the prey, to shed blood, and destroy souls, to get dishonest gain.*
>
> *And her prophets have daubed them with untempered mortar, seeing vanity, and divining lies unto them, saying Thus saith the Lord God, when the Lord hath not spoken.*
>
> *The people of the land have used oppression, and exercised robbery, and have vexed the poor and needy; yea, they have oppressed the stranger wrongfully.*
>
> *Therefore I sought for a man among them, that should stand in the hedge, and stand in the gap before me for the land, that I should not destroy it: but I found none.*
>
> *Therefore have I poured out mine indignation upon them: I have consumed them with the fire of my wrath: their own way have I recompensed upon their heads, saith the Lord God* (Ezekiel 22:26-31).

Is there a man or woman that will stand in the gap and make up the hedge, to teach and show the difference between the holy of the Lord and the profane?

Or are we all going to be stoned to death. This is the penalty for breaking the Sabbath of the Lord.

To talk about stoning this is what took place and will take place.

In Numbers.15:32-36 We have the first case of a man gathering sticks on the Sabbath day. The people that found this man brought him to Moses and the congregation. This person was held in prison until it was told what to do to this man. Moses had to inquire of the Lord as what to do. The Lord said stone the man.

The man did some kind of work on the Sabbath of the Lord, A work that got him into big time trouble.

There is coming a day that there will be a stoning and it will not be by man for breaking God's laws. It will be by the Holy One of Israel, the Lord God Almighty.

The second case, stoning was performed by God. That was when He rain fire and brimstone on Sodom and Gomorrah for their sins and transgressions against the Lord our God. We find this account in Genesis 19:24. This was done for us for an example.

> *But the same day lot went out of Sodom it rained fire and brimstone from heaven, and destroyed them* (Luke.17:29).

> *And turning the cities of Sodom and Gomorrah into ashes condemned them with an overthrow, making them an example unto those that should live ungodly* (2Peter.2:6).

There will be a stoning take place in the end, which will be by God Himself.

> *In flaming fire taking vengeance on them that know not God; who shall be punished with everlasting destruction from the presence of the Lord and from the glory of his power* (2 Thessalonians 1:8).

> *The same shall drink of the wine of the wrath of God, which is poured out without mixture into the cup of his indignation; and he shall be tormented with fire and brimstone in the presence of the holy angels, and in the presence of the Lamb* (Revelation 14:10).

What I get out of this passage is: God is doing the stoning in the presence of His holy angels and in the presence of the Lamb.

Why? Because it is God, that man keeps transgressing against through our disobedience to His word.

> *Hast thou entered into the treasures of snow? Or hast thou seen the treasures of hail, which I have reserved against the time of trouble, against the day of battle and war* (Job 38:22-23).

Here is a list of the things that are done that got people stoned and will get people stoned:

1. Anyone that transgresses the covenant of God (Deuteronomy 17:1-5, 19-20).
2. Not keeping Sabbath holy (Numbers 15:33-35).
3. Giving any seed to Molech (Leviticus 20:2).
4. Witchcraft, Familiar Spirits (Leviticus 20:6).
5. Cursing (Leviticus 24:23).
6. False teaching, Teachers, Prophets (Deuteronomy 13:1-10).
7. Wayward, rebellious child (Deuteronomy 21:18-23).
8. Adultery (Deuteronomy 22:16-29).
9. Coveting (Joshua 7:16-26).
10. Blaspheming God (1 Kings 21:10).

What's interesting is that each one of these has to do with the 10 commandments. Let us in this last generation learn to be holy and keep the things of God Holy. To keep the day of the Lord holy and not to profane his Sabbath or any of the other commandments that God has set down for us.

THE WORKS

The question, is, how is it that we profane the Sabbath? What kind of work is it that was being done that profanes the Sabbath of the Lord?

Can there be work done that does not profane, but honors God.

But the seventh day is the Sabbath of the Lord thy God: in it thou shalt not do any work, which thou may rest...

The Lord our God says that we are not to work on His holy day but to Rest.

As we look into the Bible we find two kinds of work taking place throughout the Bible. One kind of work is work that honors God and the other work does not honor God, but profanes His holy name and day.

We will look at what the Bible says about both. And how does Jesus deals with work, in the New Testament.

> *But ye shall offer an offering made by fire unto the Lord seven days: in the seventh day is a holy convocation: ye shall do no servile work therein* (Leviticus 23:8).

> *And ye shall proclaim on the selfsame day that it may be a holy convocation unto you: ye shall do no servile work therein: it shall be a statute forever in all your dwellings throughout your generations* (Leviticus 23:21).

Let us look at some definitions to help us understand what the convocation is and the servile work. As follows:

convocation – Hebrew – miqra .– (mik-rah)

- something called out

- public meeting
- assembly
- rehearsal

servile — Hebrew — abowdah.– (ab-o-dah)

- work of any kind
- bondage — bondman – bond service
- labor – laboring man
- tillage
- self serving
- menial

On the Sabbath day we are to stop our normal routine and take time out to rest and/or be with others in the worship to the Lord. The Lord gave six other days to do our slave laboring to other people. We have all heard the expression about.

I'm slaving away in the kitchen. Let's look at Luke 10:38-42 the case about Mary and Martha.

> *Now it came to pass, as they went, that he entered into a certain village: and a certain woman named Martha received him into her house.*
>
> *And she had a sister called Mary, which also sat at Jesus feet, and heard his word.*
>
> *But Martha was cumbered (burdened, busy) about much serving, and came to him, and said, Lord, dost thou not care that my sister hath left me to serve alone? Bid her therefore to help me.*
>
> *And Jesus answer and said unto her, Martha, Martha, thou art careful (fretting) and troubled (fussing) about many things.*
>
> *But one thing is needful (important): and Mary hath chosen that good part, which shall not be taken away from her* (Luke 10:38-42).

One was concerned about the things of the world and getting food for the Master, then getting food from the Master the provider of the bread. And the other chose to hear about the bread of life, Torah. This is why He told Martha that Mary chose the good part first. Not that there was anything wrong with eating. She just had her priorities backwards.

God told the Israelites when they wander in the wilderness that on the six day they would gather more bread on this day, this way they would have food to eat on the Sabbath.

> *And it came to pass, that on the six day they gather twice as much bread, two omers for one man: and all of the rulers of the congregation came and told Moses.*
>
> *And he said unto them, this is that which the Lord hath said. Tomorrow is the rest of the holy Sabbath unto the Lord: bake that which ye will bake today, and seethe that ye will seethe: and that which remaineth over lay up to be kept until morning.*
>
> *And they laid it up until morning as Moses bade: and it did not stink, neither was there any worm therein.*
>
> *And Moses said, Eat today: for today is a Sabbath unto the Lord: today ye shall not find it in the field.*
>
> *Six days ye shall gather it; but on the Sabbath, in it there shall be none.*
>
> *And it came to pass, that there went out some of the people on the seventh day for to gather, and they found none.*
>
> *And the Lord said to Moses, How long refuse ye to keep my commandments and laws* (Exodus 16:22-28)?

God is providing the food for them so they may Rest on His Holy Day, but some did not trust the Lord and went out to see for themselves, thus lacking the faith in God to be the provider. Thus, we go out and do the same things. We turn each one to our own thinking; we will improve on God's plan.

Next:

> *Ye shall kindle no fire throughout your habitations upon the Sabbath day* (Exodus 35:3).

This is stating that we are to do no major work. The fire this refers to is a consuming fire to work with in melting the different metals that they used to build the different things in the temple and other things. They would have to let this fire cool down and start over again the next day after the Sabbath.

NO COMMERCIAL WORK

Israel transgressed the laws of God. God sent them into captivity. After this time of captivity was up He brought them back into His land. But did they learn, NO. This is what takes place.

> *In those days saw I in Judah some treading wine press on the Sabbath, and bringing in sheaves, and lading asses; as also wine and grapes, and figs, and all manner of burdens, which they brought into Jerusalem on the Sabbath day: and I testified against them in the day wherein they sold victuals.*
>
> *There dwelt men of Tyre also therein, which brought fish, and all manner of ware, and sold on the Sabbath unto the children of Judah and in Jerusalem.*
>
> *Then I contended with the nobles of Judah, and said unto them, what evil thing is this that ye do, and profane the Sabbath day?*
>
> *Did not your fathers thus, and did not our God bring all this evil upon us, and upon the city? Yet ye bring more wrath upon Israel by profaning the Sabbath.*
>
> *And it came to pass, that when the gates of Jerusalem began to be dark before the Sabbath, I commanded that the gates be shut, and charged that the gates should not be opened till after the Sabbath: and some of the servants set I at the gates, that there should no burden be brought in on the Sabbath day.*
>
> *So the merchants and sellers of all kind of ware lodged without Jerusalem once or twice.*

Then I testified against them, and said unto them, why lodge ye about the wall? If ye do so again, I will lay hands on you. From that time forth came they no more on the Sabbath (Nehemiah 13:15-22).

The merchants / strangers were always trying to get Israel to do business on the Sabbath, which worked. Until one of the prophets stood up and warned the people.

Thus said the Lord unto me Go and stand in the gate of the children of the people, whereby the kings of Judah came in, and by the which they go out, and in all of the gates of Jerusalem;

And say unto them, Hear ye the word of the Lord; ye kings of Judah and all of Judah, and all the inhabitants of Jerusalem, that enter the gates:

Thus saith the Lord; Take heed to yourselves, and bear no burden on the Sabbath day, nor bring it in by the gates of Jerusalem;

Neither carry forth a burden out of your houses on the Sabbath day, neither do ye any work, but hallow the Sabbath day as I commanded your fathers.

But they obeyed not, neither inclined their ear, but made their neck stiff, that they might not hear, nor receive instruction.

And it shall come to pass, if ye diligently hearken unto me saith the Lord to bring no burden through the gates of the city on the Sabbath day, but hallow the Sabbath day, to do no work therein;

Then shall there enter into the gates of this city kings and princes sitting upon the throne of David, riding in chariots and on horses, they, and their princes, the men of Judah, and the inhabitants of Jerusalem: and this city will remain for ever.

And they shall come from the cities of Judah, and the places of Jerusalem, and from the land of Benjamin, and from the plain, and from the mountains, and from the

> *south, bringing burnt offerings, and incense, and bringing sacrifices of praise, unto the house of the Lord.*
>
> *But if ye will not hearken unto me to hallow the Sabbath day and not to bear a burden, even entering in at the gates of Jerusalem on the Sabbath day; then will I kindle a fire in the gates thereof, and it shall devour the palaces of Jerusalem, and it (fire) it shall not be quenched* (Jeremiah 17:19-27).

In these passages the Lord is very clear about working on His holy day. He says that if we don't stop and commune with Him then He will kindle a fire that will not be quenched.

This fire is the wrath of God being poured out on all the transgressors of His laws and commandments.

> *Thus saith the Lord God: Behold, I will kindle a fire in thee, and it shall devour every green tree in thee, and every dry tree: the flaming flame shall not be quenched, and all faces from the south to the north shall be burned therein. And all flesh shall see that I the Lord have kindled it: it shall not be quenched* (Ezekiel 20:47-48).
>
> *Therefore thus saith the Lord God; Behold mine anger and my fury shall be poured out upon this place, upon man, and upon beast, and upon the trees of the field, and upon the fruit of the ground; and it shall burn, and shall not be quenched* (Jeremiah 7:20).
>
> *For it is the day of the Lord's vengeance, and the year of recompenses for the controversy of Zion. And the streams thereof shall be turned into pitch, and the dust thereof into brimstone, and the land thereof shall become burning pitch. It shall not be quenched night or day; the smoke there of shall go up forever: from generation to generation it shall lie waste; none shall pass through it forever* (Isaiah 34:8-10).

As these passages indicate the Lord is going to start a fire that will burn forever, and it will start in Jerusalem and go global and burn all of His transgressors.

THE COMPLAINT

Complaining, people love to complain, some are not happy unless they are complaining about something or someone. This is the case for the merchants in the time of Amos. The merchants did not want to follow the rules that the Lord had set down. These merchants were dishonest.

> *Saying, When will the new moon be gone, that we may sell corn? And the Sabbath, that we may set forth wheat, making the ephod small, and the shekel (dollar) great, and falsifying the balances by deceit?*
>
> *That we may buy the poor for silver, and the needy for a pair of shoes; yea, and sell the refuse of the wheat* (Amos 8:5-6)?

We all complain when the Lord says something that we do not like. So we begin to do things our ways. Anything to make a buck, cheat our neighbors and the poor and needy. We make up our own rules then try to bind them on everyone else. We don't like being bound by the Lord, but we sure do like putting other people under our bondage. We are like the people that Jesus deals with when He walked the earth, as we will look at soon, But first the Lord's answers.

> *The Lord hath sworn by the Excellency of Jacob, Surely I will never forget any of their works* (Amos 8:7).

Also read the rest of Amos 8:8-12 for the rest of the answer. The Lord will cause a famine in the land for the true word of God and none shall find it. Because the word hast been polluted by so many wolfs in sheep clothing.

The Lord has made it very clear about buying and selling on His holy day the Sabbath of the Lord. But there are people that can't wait until Sabbath is over. We go about our own ways and get things through buying and selling.

To make it more clear from the Lord.

> *And they came to Jerusalem: and Jesus went into the temple, and began to cast out them that sold and bought in the temple, and overthrew the tables of the moneychangers, and the seats of them that sold doves;*
>
> *And would not suffer that any man carry any vessel through the temple.*
>
> *And he taught, saying unto them, is it not written, my house shall be called of all nations the house of prayer? But ye have made it a den of thieves.*
>
> *And the scribe and chief priests heard it, and sought how they might destroy him: for they feared him, because all the people were astonished at his doctrine* (Mark.11:15-18).

The Lord has made it very clear in these passages we need to shut down the buying and selling on His Holy Day. The only place, which gets shut down to a point, is in Jerusalem in the Jewish sections of the city. The same command is to all of us, both Jew and Gentile who say that they know God.

Let us turn to the other kind of works that were being done on the Sabbath.

WORK OF THE SABBATH

There are works which the Lord God commanded the priest to do on the Sabbath, which the Lord does not consider work. Let us look at some of the things they did on the Sabbath.

> *And the priest shall look on him the seventh day: and behold, if the plague in his sight be at a stay, and the plague spread not in the skin; then the priest shall shut him up seven more days.*
>
> *And the priest shall look on him again the seventh day: and, behold, if the plague be somewhat dark, and the plague spread not to the skin, the priest shall pronounce him clean: it is but a scab: and he shall wash his clothes, and be clean* (Leviticus 13:5-6).

The priest would examine the people on the seventh day to see if they were clean or unclean and then he would prescribe what the person should do. Read Leviticus chapters 13 and 14 to see what all their priest would do.

In Numbers 19 this deals with the unclean becoming clean again and the process they would go through. Take note of this verse, Numbers 19:19

> *And the clean person shall sprinkle upon the unclean on the third day, and on the seventh day: and on the seventh day he shall purify himself, and wash his clothes, and bathe himself in water, and shall be clean at even.*

This is also a shadow of baptism mention in the New Testament, of how it is not just an outward cleansing, but also an inward cleansing of the soul.

The like figure whereunto baptism doth also save us (not the putting away the filth of the flesh, but the answer of a good conscience toward God (1Peter 3:21).

During the appointed feast Israel would offer animal sacrifices to the Lord.

And on the seventh day seven bullocks, two rams, and fourteen lambs of the first year without blemish:

And their meat offering and their drink offering for the bullocks, for the rams, and for the lambs, shall be according to their number, after the manner.

And one goat for a sin offering; beside the continual burnt offering, his meat offering, and his drink offering (Numbers 29:32-34).

This takes a tremendous amount of effort to do, to prepare the animal for sacrifice. This is work, but a command that pleased God. What kinds of sacrifice do we do for the Lord God on His holy day?

Consider Romans 12:1-2:

I beseech you therefore brethren, by the mercies of God, that ye present your bodies a living sacrifice, holy, acceptable unto God, which is your reasonable service.

And be not conformed to this world: but be ye transformed by the renewing of your mind, that ye may prove what is that good, and acceptable, and perfect, will of God.

They would prepare the show bread on the Sabbath.

...were over the showbread, to prepare it every Sabbath. (1 Chronicles 9:32).

After the people prepare the showbread they would put in the sanctuary.

We also have showbread that we put into the sanctuary every Sabbath.

There are two kinds:

- The word of the living God, which we read and study and listen to each Sabbath.
- By eating and drinking of the bread and fruit of the vine, we put it into the sanctuary each Sabbath. The sanctuary is our body or the temple, which the Holy Spirit dwells in if we are a believer.

BATTLE ON THE SABBATH

Many times God would have His people go into battle on His holy day to defeat His enemy.

> *And they pitched one over against the other seven days. And so it was that in the seventh day the battle was joined: and the children of Israel slew of the Syrians a hundred thousand footmen in one day* (1 Kings 20:29).

Have you heard of the city of Jericho and how it fell in Joshua 6:1-27? We will look at verses 4 and 15.

> *And seven priests shall bear before the ark seven trumpets of ram's horns: and the seventh day ye shall compass the city seven times around the priest shall blow with the trumpets* (Joshua 6:4).

> *And it came to pass on the seventh day that they rose early about dawning of the day, and compassed the city after the same manner seven times* (Joshua 6:15).

The question arises: I thought we are to Rest? We are to Rest from our labors, of everything, which is self-serving to our own needs, but we are to do the Lord's bidding and work which pleases Him on His holy day.

What is the saying when it comes to Friday, we say thank God it's Friday and the weekend comes.

Friday night is the big night, because this is the beginning of God's Sabbath, which is to start in the homes with the families and friends, in which we bless the Lord and each other, with sharing the WORD of the Lord.

Where are we on the Sabbath of the Lord, honoring the Sabbath, or slaving away at work that we can put off until another day?

Also, we see Israel do battle in the land on the Sabbath, to defend the land and the city of Jerusalem, Trying to keep the enemies of God at bay. In many cases we have seen God fight for Israel in the past and the enemy would be defeated.

JESUS AND THE SABBATH

We will see that the Jesus does a lot of God's mighty works on His holy day. Jesus gives us the examples on what can be done on His Sabbath. And how He deals with the Scribes and Pharisees as they are trying to bind manmade traditions on the creator. Many times they forget what their forefathers were to do.

Teaches

The Lord teaches.

> *And they went into Capernaum: and straightway on the Sabbath day he enters into the synagogue, and taught.*
>
> *And they were astonished at his doctrine: for he taught them as one that had authority, and not as the scribes* (Mark 1:21-22).
>
> *And when the Sabbath day was come, he began to teach in the synagogue: and many hearing him were astonished, saying, from whence hath this man these things* (Mark 6:2)?
>
> *And he came to Nazareth, where he had been brought up; and as his custom was, he went into the synagogue on the Sabbath day, and stood up and read* (Luke 4:16).
>
> *And he came down to Capernaum, a city of Galilee, and taught them on the Sabbath day.* (Luke 4:31).
>
> *And it came to pass also on another Sabbath, that he entered into the synagogue and taught: and there was a man whose right hand was withered* (Luke 6:6).

Heals

The Lord heals.

> *And, behold, there was a man which had is hand withered. And they asked him, saying, is it lawful to heal on the Sabbath days, that they might accuse him. And he said unto them, What man shall there be among you, that shall have one sheep, and if it fall into a pit on the Sabbath day, will he not lay hold on it, and lift it out?*
>
> *How much then is a man better than a sheep? Wherefore it is lawful to do well on the Sabbath days.*
>
> *Then saith he to the man, Stretch forth thine hand. And he stretched it forth and it was restored whole, like the other,*
>
> *Then the Pharisees went out, and held council against him, how they might destroy him* (Matthew 12:10-14, Mark. 3:1-6, Luke.6:6-11).
>
> *And he was teaching in one of the synagogues on the Sabbath.*
>
> *And behold, there was a woman, which had a spirit of infirmity eighteen years, and was bowed together, and could no wise lift up herself.*
>
> *And when Jesus saw her, he called her to him, and said to unto her, Woman; thou art loosed from thine infirmity.*
>
> *And he laid hands on her: and immediately she was made straight, and glorified God.*
>
> *And the rulers of the synagogue answered with indignation, because that Jesus had healed on the Sabbath day and said unto the people, There six days in which men ought to work: in them therefore come and be healed, and not on the Sabbath day.*
>
> *The Lord then answer him, and said, Thou hypocrite, doth not each one of you on the Sabbath loose his ox or his ass from the stall, and lead him away for watering?*

And ought not this woman, being a daughter of Abraham, whom Satan hath bound, lo, these eighteen years, be loosed from this bond on the Sabbath day?

And when he had said these things, all his adversaries were ashamed: and all of the people rejoiced for all the glorious things that were done by him (Luke 13:10-17).

Many other healings the Lord did on the Sabbath.

John 5 Jesus heals a man at the pool of Bethesda. v. 9, 10 and it was the Sabbath day

John 9 Jesus heals the blind man. vs14. It was the Sabbath day when Jesus made the clay, and opens his eyes.

Luke 14 Jesus heal man with dropsy

Eating

The Lord eats food with people.

*And it came to pass on the second Sabbath after the first, that he went through the corn fields; and his disciples plucked the ears of the corn, and did eat, rubbing them in their hands (*Luke 6:1, Mark 2:23).

And it came to pass, as he went into the house of one of the Pharisees to eat bread on the Sabbath day, that they watch him (Luke14:1).

Jesus is saying it is good, to do good on God's holy day. The Pharisees were always trying to make their own rules as to what the people could do or not do. They were always changing ways on many teaching of Moses and the forefathers. So they would not break the commandments. Or they would just do their own thing no matter what.

Rested

The common people would follow the commands of the Lord.

And that day was the preparation, and the Sabbath drew on. And they returned, and prepared spices and ointment; and rested the Sabbath day according to the commandment (Luke 23:54, 56).

Many of the people would Rest according to the command of God and do no work. How about us? How do we keep the Sabbath?

THE DOMINION

In the beginning when God created all life on the face of the earth, then He created man and tells man to be caretakers of the ground and that he had the right to one thing called dominion, he, man would be over the other creatures.

> *And God blessed them, and God said unto them, Be fruitful, and multiply, and have dominion over the fish of the sea, and over the fowl of the air, and over every living thing that moveth upon the earth* (Genesis 1:28).

Also see Psalms, Chapter 8.

What is dominion?

- right of lordship
- supreme authority or control; sovereignty: rule

This is the thing that men throughout all ages have tried to have is dominion over everything and everyone they possibly can. Through any means they can to do it. Even the Devil himself is trying to gain complete control over everyone's lives through any means possible.

To say the worst he is doing a good job at it.

But, there is only one person and one thing that has dominion over every man and everything.

- It is the Lord God, creator of heaven and earth.

> *Thy kingdom is an everlasting kingdom, and thy dominion endureth thought out all generations* (Psalms 145:13).

Bless ye the Lord, all ye host: ye ministers that do his pleasure. Bless the Lord, all his works in all places of his dominion: bless the Lord, O my soul (Psalms 103:21-22).

He shall have dominion also from sea to sea, and from river unto the ends of the earth (Psalms 72:8).

- The seventh day Sabbath

When God came down on Mount Sinai, He established His covenant with Man. And Man agreed.

And Moses came and told the people all the words of the Lord, and all the judgments; and all the people answered with one voice, and said, All the words the Lord hath said we will do (Exodus 24:3).

When the Lord came down and spoke He made His Holy Sabbath very clear.

Thou camest down also upon the Mount Sinai, and spakest with them from heaven, and gavest them right judgments, and true laws, good statutes and commandments.

And maketh known unto them thy Holy Sabbath, and commandedest them precepts, statutes, and laws by the hand of Moses thy servant (Nehemiah 9:13-14).

The Lord has supreme dominion over everything and everyone, notice His response.

For the Son of man is Lord even of the Sabbath day (Matthew 12:28).

Therefore the Son of man is Lord also of the Sabbath (Luke.2:28).

The Lord tells man what his position is in relation to His holy day.

And he said to them, the Sabbath was made for man and not man for the Sabbath (Mark 2:27).

The Sabbath is to have dominion over the man. To stop, rest and reflect on the Lord. But man has gotten everything backwards and is trying to control God and His holy days. We the creation have been trying to worship ourselves and not the creator, which the devil even has done, and is getting everyone else to do the same.

The Lord is Holy and His Day is Holy, it is time we begin to put this into the right prospective and quit trying to have dominion over everything and Let God have dominion over us and the way we live.

THE OXEN FACTOR

There are things that a person just hast to do. There is no way getting around it. The car has a flat. You're getting ready to have a baby and the baby won't wait. If you raise animals you have to feed them. The Lord had to deal with these problems.

> *The Lord answered him, and said, Thou hypocrite, doth each one of you on the Sabbath loose his ox or his ass from the stall, and lead him away to watering* (Luke 13:15)?

> *And answered them, saying, which of you shall have an ass or ox fallen into the pit, and will not straightway pull him out on the Sabbath day* (Luke 14:5)?

> *And he said unto them, What man shall there be among you, that shall have one sheep, and if it fall into a pit on the Sabbath day, will he not lay hold on it, and lift it out* (Matthew 12:11-12)?

How much then is a man better than a sheep? Wherefore it is lawful to do well on the Sabbath days.

Many of the Pharisees all the time were trying to accuse Jesus of breaking the Sabbath, but He knew the rules of the Sabbath better than the religious leaders, because the religious leaders had their own rules and commandments whereby to impose them on the other people and mainly the Lord of the Sabbath. So the Lord puts them in their place.

> *Did not Moses give you the law, and yet none of you keepeth the law? Why go ye about to kill me?*

> *The people answered and said Thou hast a devil: who goeth about to kill thee.*

> *Jesus answered and said unto them, I have done one work, and ye all marvel.*
>
> *Moses therefore gave unto you circumcision; (not because it is of Moses, but the fathers;) and ye on the Sabbath day circumcise a man.*
>
> *If a man on the Sabbath day receive circumcision, that the Law of Moses should not be broken; are ye angry at me, because I have made a man every whit whole on the Sabbath day?*
>
> *Judge not according to appearance, but righteous judgment* (John 7:19-24).

One thing that the Lord wants us to shut down the commercial end of doing business and spends time in rest, with our family and friends and in His Word.

But there are those things that will always have to be done at times, such as feeding your animals, feeding your kids.

Then there are the times of emergency that have to be done when someone needs help and it cannot wait. These things like this are consider acts of kindness. Be it medical, fire, police, etc. When there is not an emergency then we / they should take off also, even though we / they may be subject to call. Life and death will at times take the priority over other things. Example: if you were having a heart attack and about to die you hope someone was around to help or get some help.

Jesus answered the leaders by saying how much better is a man than an animal.

The ox in the ditch is not trying to make a buck on the Sabbath, or going shopping to spend money, because there is a sale on at one of the stores. These are things that please us and not God.

But now if someone is in need and you went to the store to get them some food to eat or clothes to wear, because they need them. This would be doing unto the least of these and you have done it to me.

In Isaiah 58:13,14 God said to refrain from doing our own pleasure on His holy day and do His pleasure

How do we measure up to this so far?

Let's take a look at the people hearing the Law of God in the time of Ezra and Nehemiah. This was when they began to return to Jerusalem after the exile.

Ezra reads from the book of the law of God to the people.

> *So they read in the book in the Law of God distinctly, and gave sense, and caused them to understand the reading.*
>
> *This day is holy unto the Lord your God; morn not, nor weep. For All the people wept, when they heard the words of the law* (Nehemiah 8:8-9).

After the people heard and understood the words of God this is their response, because they sealed the covenant of God.

> *And all they that had separated themselves from the people of the lands unto the law of God, their wives, their sons, and their daughters, every one having knowledge, and having understanding;*
>
> *They clave to their brethren, their nobles, and entered into a curse (vow), and into an oath, to walk in God's Law, which was given by Moses the servant of God, and to observe and do all the commandments of the Lord our Lord, and his judgments and his statutes;*
>
> *And if the people of the land bring ware or any victuals on the Sabbath day to sell, that we would not buy it of them on the Sabbath, or on the holy day* (Nehemiah 10:28-29,31).

What do we do? Buy and sell or wait until the next day.

Have we separated ourselves to the Word of God or are we still playing in the sand pit and drinking milk from the bottle. Or are we ready to take on the strong food and drink, such as meat and potatoes. See the strong word of God is the meat and potatoes for those of us that are ready to handle the truths and not the lies.

Let's see what Paul says about milk and meat.

> *And I, brethren, could not speak unto you as unto spiritual, but as unto carnal, even as babes in Christ.*
>
> *I have fed you with milk, and not with meat: for hitherto ye are not able to bear it, neither yet now are ye able* (1 Corinthians 3:1-2).
>
> *For when for the time ye ought to be teachers, ye have need that one teach you again which be the first principles of the oracles of God; and are become such as have need of milk and not strong meat.*
>
> *For every one that useth milk is unskillful in the word of righteousness: for he is a babe.*
>
> *But strong meat belongeth to them that are full age, even those who by reason of use have their senses exercised to discern both good and evil* (Hebrews 5:12-14).

We can also say to discern between the Holy and the profane.

THE CHURCH AND THE SABBATH

As we come to the book of Acts of the Apostles, we come to what some call the church age (Acts 1:9-11). Before Jesus ascended to heaven He tells His disciples that in a little while they would receive power from on high. In Acts 2 they were in the upper room on the day of Pentecost when they receive this power from on high and the Holy Spirit came on them and in them.

Now, the question is, when the church has its jump-start in Acts, what is the relationship of the church and the Sabbath?

Did the Sabbath change from the seventh day of the week to the first day of the week?

Did the Apostles receive authority to change what God set apart?

Do we have the right to change what God set apart?

As we journey through the book of Acts, we find what the book of Acts says about the church in respect to God's Holy Day.

The book of Acts was written somewhere around 62 AD. It covers parts of Paul's four missionary journeys, and covering 30 years of history of the early church. If anything was going to change it will take place in this book, the book of action of the early believers.

From Paul's conversion to his first missionary journey were several years.

Paul's conversion was around 31 AD. And his first missionary journey was from 45 to 48 AD. As we join Paul in his first missionary journey in Acts 13 let's see what is taking place.

> *But when they departed from Perga they came to Antioch in Pisidia, and went into the synagogue on the Sabbath day, and sat down.*

> *And after the reading of the law and the prophets the rulers of the synagogue sent unto them saying, ye men and brethren, if ye have any word of exhortation for the people, say on.*
>
> *Then Paul stood up, and beckoning with his hand said, Men of Israel, and ye that fear God, give audience* (Acts 13:14-16).
>
> *For they that dwell in Jerusalem, and their rulers, because they knew him not, nor yet the voices of the prophets, which are read every Sabbath day (*Acts13:27).
>
> *And when the Jews were gone out of the synagogue, the Gentiles besought that these words might be preached to them the next Sabbath* (Acts13:42).

In this passage the Gentiles come into the synagogue on the Sabbath to hear the Word of God. They did not have a different day to worship on. As we come to know, then we would give up our ways for the ways of God.

> *And the next Sabbath day came almost the whole city together to hear the word of God* (Acts13:44).

It says that the **WHOLE CITY** came together on the Sabbath day that is both Jew and Gentiles to hear the word of the Lord, On the day that the Lord had sanctified as His day of Rest. Now look what happens.

> *But when the Jews saw the multitudes, they were filled with envy, (jealousy)* (Acts 13:45).

Now look at Romans 11:10-11:

> *Let their (Israel, Jews) eyes be darkened, that they may not see, and bow down their back always. I say then, Have they stumbled that they should fall? God forbid: but rather through their fall salvation is come to the Gentiles, for to provoke them (Jews) to Jealousy.*

So how do you provoke someone to jealousy? You do the same things they are doing or should be doing, because they have had it all along and take it for granted. And now you come along and do the same things and it really burns their bridges and lights a fire under them to make them more zealous for what they had taken for granted.

Let's continue on:

> *For Moses of old time hath in every city them that preach him, being read in the synagogues every Sabbath day. Then pleased it the apostles and elders, with the whole church* (Acts 15:21-22).

> *And on the Sabbath day we went out of the city by a riverside, where prayer was wont (usually) to be made; and we sat down, and spake unto the women which resorted thither* (Acts 16:13).

> *Now when they had passed through Amphipolis and Apolonia they came to Thessalonica, where was a synagogue of the Jews: And Paul, as his manner was, went in unto them, and three Sabbath days reasoned with them out of the scripture* (Acts 17:1-2).

> *And he reasoned in the synagogue every Sabbath, and persuaded the Jews and the Greeks* (Acts 18:4).

In the book of Acts the Sabbath is still the same day, the seventh day, not the first day. We go to Matt 28:1 *In the end of the Sabbath, as it began to dawn toward the first day of the week*, this shows the different between the two days. Also Mark 16:1-2. But you say what about Acts 20:7, well let's look at this verse and compare it with some others in Acts.

> *And upon the first day of the week, when the disciples were come together to break bread, Paul preached unto them, ready to depart on the morrow, and he continue his speech until midnight.*

A few things that we need to remember:

How does God figure time?

God said in Genesis that from evening and the morning was a day. Not midnight to midnight or sunrise to sunrise. See Genesis 1:1-31

The seventh day of the week had just ended and it was getting dark. As we read on in vs. 8 there were many lights in the upper chamber. It was not practical of them to have lights on in the day, being they had to light them and put oil in them.

To break bread. This is to eat.

The disciples would get together every night and break bread, (eat). Notice verse 11 and had broken bread, and eaten, and talked a long while....Let's go to Acts 2

> *And they continued steadfastly in the apostle's doctrine and fellowship, and breaking of bread, and prayers* (Acts2:42).

To put in our modern terms they came together and had dinner on the grounds or fellowship meal, where everyone comes together and shares with one another and talks.

> *And they continuing daily with one accord in the temple, and breaking bread from house to house, did eat their meat with gladness and singleness of heart* (Acts 20:46).

Notice the house to house, some were having other people over to their home after work, if you will, and they would eat dinner, or maybe they would get together for lunch.

Another thing to notice is they continue daily. They were studying the word and discussing it every day. We can come together every day also and go to all kinds of meetings, but we still need to set God's day apart and do what He has said to do. On the other six days we can meet and then go about doing our own business. But on God's Holy Day we do those things that please Him.

Paul was getting ready to leave and go on a voyage, so he would not be back in that area for a while; In this case they were having a farewell dinner for Paul. It's like when your congregation has a guest speaker over we have this big potluck dinner after service. This is what they were having but only it was Saturday night, not Sunday afternoon.

From looking at the book of Acts the Sabbath has never changed. But when did it change and who changed it?

> *The earth also is defiled under the inhabitants thereof; because they have transgressed the laws, changed the ordinance, broken the everlasting covenant* (Isaiah 24:5).
>
> *...and think to change times and laws* (Daniel 7:25).

Who changed the Sabbath, we the inhabitants of the earth, by doing so we transgress the laws of the Most High God?

THE NEW HEAVEN AND EARTH

> *For as the new heaven and the new earth, which I will make, shall remain before me, saith the Lord, so shall your seed and your name remain.*
>
> *And it shall come to pass, that from one new moon to another, and from one Sabbath to another, shall all flesh come to worship before me saith the Lord.*
>
> *And they shall go forth, and look upon the carcasses of the men that have transgressed against me: for their worm shall not die, neither shall their fire be quenched; and they shall be abhorring unto all flesh* (Isaiah 66:22-24).

This is the day of the Lord the seventh day the Sabbath Rest that we are to be rehearsing for. If we do not enter into the Rest now in this life then we may be one of the carcasses of the transgressor and will not be learning from the Lord Himself. By studying the rest of the passage we will see, this is the day of the Lord's wrath, also His second coming; connect this with many other passages about the day of the Lord or the wrath of God.

Along with going up each Sabbath and worship the Lord, we will go up each year to the feast of tabernacles.

> *And it shall come to pass, that every one that is left of all the nations which came against Jerusalem shall even go up from year to year to worship the King, the Lord of host, and to keep the feast of tabernacles* (Zechariah 14:16).

Zechariah 14 deals with the day of wrath, of the Lord and the great battle that is yet to take place at Jerusalem when all the nations come up against her and the Lord in turn will fight for Jerusalem and his people.

So the Lord did not change the Sabbath, we are still going up to worship Him in the next millennium, at Jerusalem, on the Sabbath and on the feast of Tabernacles.

THE SIGN

Signs are everywhere that we go. Each sign is an indication of something or someone belonging to someone or something else. We have signs to tell us to stop and to yield, signs to tell how fast to go. Then we have signs and symbols in the sports as to what team that we are rooting for or which team that you belong with.

This is the same way with God. He has a sign that will tell which people belong to him and which people don't. So let us look at the word to see what the sign or distinguishing mark of His people.

> *And the Lord said to Moses, Say to the people of Israel, You shall keep my Sabbaths, for this is a sign between me and you throughout your generations, that you may know that I, the Lord, sanctify you. You shall keep my Sabbath, because it is holy for you; everyone who profanes it shall be put to death. It is a sign between me and the people of Israel that in six days the Lord made the heavens and the earth, and on the seventh day he rested, and was refreshed* (Exodus 31:12-14,17).

> *Moreover I gave them my Sabbaths, as a sign between them, and me that they might know that I the Lord sanctify them* (Ezekiel 20:12).

> *And hallow my Sabbaths that they may be a sign between you, and me that you may know that I the Lord am your God* (Ezekiel 20:20).

This is the sign between God and His children, which sets them apart from the rest of the world and nations. But what is it that His children do?

> *But the children rebelled against me: they did not walk in my statutes, and were not careful to observe my ordinances, by whose observance man shall live; they profaned my Sabbaths* (Ezekiel 20:21).

We are the children of God.

We belong to Him and are to keep His Sabbaths, but what we have done is rebelled against the Father by doing our own ways. Any one that is born again, now becomes part of Israel and heirs of the promises made to Abraham. When we have a rebellious spirit then it shows that we do not belong to the Father but prefer to belong to the wicked one Satan.

Whom do we want to belong to God the Father or to Satan? Submit therefore to God and live or rebel and die, where do we stand?

Shall we learn to keep the Sabbaths of God and make them a delight?

THE TEST

Have you ever taken a test in your life, of course you have. These tests are to see if we have studied the lessons. When we were in high school the teachers would give these test, a lot of times we would take some of the test and sweat them not knowing if we pass or not, some knew that we failed because we did not study the right information, and sometimes we half studied, thinking that we could slide by.

There is a test going on right now in our lives, some will pass the test and many others will fail the test. And it's because we are not studying or listening to the right teachers. It does not matter about the teacher if you rightly divide the word of God in proper study. But many of us just listen to the preacher and take in just whatever he says without checking it out for ourselves, and then will be led astray. Many are being led astray as it is already.

What does the Lord have to say about the testing or the proving ground?

> *Then the Lord said to Moses, Behold I will rain bread from heaven for you; and the people shall go out and gather a days portion every day, that I many prove them, whether they will walk in my law or not* (Exodus 16:4, RSV[1]).

> *And Moses said to the people Do not fear; for God has come to prove you, and that the fear of him may be before your eyes, that you may not sin* (Exodus 20:20).

---

[1] Revised Standard Version of the Bible New Testament section, copyright 1952 by the Division of Christian Education, a National Council of Churches of Christ in the United States of America.

And you shall remember all the way which the Lord your God has led you these forty years in the wilderness that he might humble you, testing you to know what was in your heart, whether you would keep his commandments or not (Deuteronomy 8:2).

...that he might humble you and test you, to do you good in the end (Deuteronomy 8:16).

In the whole land says the Lord, two thirds shall be cut off and perish, and one third shall be left alive. And I will put this third into the fire, and refine them as one refines silver, and test them as gold is tested. They will call on my name, and I will answer them. I will say, they are my people: and they will say, the Lord is my God (Zechariah 13:8-9).

If a prophet arises among you, or a dreamer of dreams, and gives you a sign or a wonder, and the sign or wonder which he tells you comes to pass, and if he says, Let us go after other gods, which you have not known, and to serve them, you shall not listen to the words of that prophet or to that dreamer of dreams; for the Lord your God is testing you, to know whether you love the Lord your God with all your heart and with all your soul. You shall walk after the Lord your God and fear him, and keep his commandments and obey his voice, and shall serve him and cleave to him. But that prophet or dreamer of dreams shall be put to death, because he has taught rebellion against the Lord your God (Deuteronomy 13:1-5).

God's word will stand forever; none will be done away until heaven and earth pass away. Are we passing the tests or are we failing the tests. The Sabbath of the Lord God is a test for us to pass; it is also a command from God. Where do we, stand in this test so far?

Let us stand only on the words of God. This is not the only test God is putting us through; there are many more tests the Lord has that are in His commandments. They consist of His laws, statutes, and judgments, found throughout the word of the Lord.

THE PROMISE

Promises, Promises is what God says He will do when we do what He asks us to do. He promises to bless us when we follow His will. What are the promises that will happen when we take hold of His Holy Day the seventh day Sabbath (Rev.2:26)? And keep His deeds unto the end.

> *Even unto them will I will give in mine house and within my wall a place and a name better than of sons and of daughters: I will give them an everlasting name, that shall not be cut off.* (Isaiah 56:5).
>
> *...make them joyful in my house of prayer...*(Isaiah 56:7).
>
> *....I will cause thee to ride upon the high places of the earth, and feed thee with the heritage of Jacob...*(Isaiah 58:14).

Some of the other promises, when we overcome the things of the world and walk uprightly in His ways.

> *I will grant to eat of the tree of life, which in the paradise of God* (Revelation 2:7).
>
> *.... I will give of the hidden manna,...I will give him a white stone, and a new name written on stone* (Revelation 2:17).
>
> *...I will give authority over nations...*(Revelation 2:26).
>
> *...shall be clothed in white garments....*
>
> *...I will not erase his name from the book of life...*
>
> *...I will confess his name before the father and his angels* (Revelation 3:5).

To receive these promises and blessing all we need to do is the Father's will.

> *Not everyone that saith unto me, Lord, Lord, shall enter into the kingdom of heaven; but he that doeth the will of my Father, which is heaven* (Matthew 7:21).

THE REST OF HEBREWS EXAMINED

Rest, we all look for Rest that is the Rest in God. When will we find Rest in God?

We will now look at Rest and belief and how they relate to each other. Starting with Hebrews 3:17, we read in this chapter, where God brought the people out of Egypt by Moses and they wandered around in the wilderness for forty years. The people were always testing God even though they saw His mighty hand for forty years. The people were always grieving The Father.

> *But with whom was he grieved forty years? Was it not with them that had sinned, whose carcasses fell in the wilderness?*
>
> *And to whom swear he that they should not enter into his rest, but to them that believed not.*
>
> *So we see that they could not enter in because of unbelief* (Hebrews 3:17-19).

Here we have a people that saw the mighty hand of God do wonders for them. They would turn and do their own thing, they did not believe. What is it that they didn't believe? They did not believe what God told them to do and how to live. God set forth standards for His people to live by, the same standards for us to live by. These people die in the wilderness because of their unbelief.

> *But the house of Israel rebelled against me in the wilderness: they walked not in My statutes, and they despised My judgments, which if a man do, he shall even live in them; and my Sabbaths they greatly polluted: then*

I said, I would pour out my fury upon them in the wilderness, to consume them (Ezekiel 20:13).

This is what Israel died for in the wilderness, this is their unbelief, by not keeping the statutes and judgments and Sabbaths of God. Will this happen to us also, by the same unbelief in not keeping the commandments of God.

As we look into Hebrews Chapter 4, I use some other translations to help give a better understanding of the verses.

Hebrews 4:1 *Let us therefore fear, lest, a promise being left us of entering into his rest* (Hebrews 4:1).

...we shall enter God's rest (TCNT[2]).

...any of you should seem to come short of it (ASV[3]).

For unto us was the gospel preached, as well as unto them: but the word preached did not profit them, not being mixed with faith in them that heard it (v 2).

...because they were not by faith made one with those who heeded it (WMS[4]).

For we who have believed do enter into his rest (v. 3).

There were and are many people that will enter God's Rest because they believe what God has said in His laws, statutes and judgments, thus obeying what He said for us to do. Many of us do not enter into His Rest because we don't really believe what He has said. We are a true believer when we are a doer of the laws of God, not just a hearer or a giver of lip service to God.

For he spake in a certain place of the seventh day on this wise, And God did rest the seventh day from all his works (v. 4).

---

[2] The Twentieth Century New Testament, Moody Bible Institute.

[3] American Standard Version, 1901, Thomas Nelson and Sons.

[4] The New Testament: A Translation in the Language of the People (Charles B. Williams), Copyright 1937 by Bruce Humphries, Inc. copyright renewed 1965 by Edith S. Williams.

And God rested from all his works on the seventh day (MOF[5]).

...because in one place he said about the seventh day (BECK[6])

...he says elsewhere in the scriptures (PHI[7])

for, in a passage referring to the seventh day, you will find these words (TCNT).

And in this place again, if they shall enter in my rest (v.5).

If they shall enter into the rest of me (Greek Inter[8]).

He has also declared (WEY[9]).

The Question, now is, where is this certain place?

To get the answer of the certain place we must turn to Exodus 19 where Israel has come to Mount Sinai and camped there. Then Moses went up to God on the Mount. Then in Exodus 20 we read where God speaks and brings forth His commandments. One of the commandments is the seventh day that He spoke to all of Israel.

Now we go to the book of Nehemiah 9 It says,

Thou camest down also upon Mount Sinai and spakest with them from heaven...

And madest known unto them thy Holy Sabbath (Nehemiah 9:13-14).

---

[5] The New Testament: A New Translation (James Moffatt), Copyright 1964 by James Moffat. Harper and Row Publishers, Inc. and Hooder and Stoughton, Ltd.

[6] The New Testament in the Language of Today (William Beck), copyright 1963 by Concordia Publishing House.

[7] The New Testament in Modern English (J.B. Phillips) copyright 1960 by J. B. Phillips, Geoffrey Bles, Ltd.

[8] Greek Interlinear: Parallel New Testament in Greek and English, copyright 1975, Zondervan Publishing Company.

[9] The New Testament Modern Speech (Richard Frances Weymouth), Harper and Row Publishers, Inc. and James Clarke and Company, Ltd.

So the certain place is Mount Sinai in which God spoke to all of Israel about His Holy Sabbath the seventh day.

> *Seeing therefore it remaineth that some must enter therein, and they to whom it was first preached enter not in because of unbelief* (v 6).
>
> *...failed to enter in because of disobedience* (ASV).

There will be many that will enter into God's Rest when they learn of His Rest, then believe and obey what He has said. Samuel told King Saul that it was better to obey than to sacrifice. To us it is better that we obey than to do our own thing.

> *Again, he limited a certain day, saying in David, Today, after so long a time; as it is said, Today if ye will hear his voice, harden not your hearts* (v. 7)
>
> *...he again defined a certain day* (ASV).
>
> *Again he maketh a certain day* (RHM[10]).
>
> *Again he designates a certain day* (ABUV[11]).
>
> *Again he sets a certain day* (RSV).

Looking at the different translations we see God has set aside a certain day to be His day of Rest. What day of Rest is His day, look back at verse 4, And God Rested on the seventh day, and all of us that Rest on His day also enter into His Rest. This is the day that He sanctifies in the beginning, and then wrote into the tablets of stone on the mountain.

What does it mean to limit a certain day?

To limit something is to:

- that which confines or bounds
- a boundary
- a fixed line or point beyond which extent is not possible

---

[10] The Emphasized New Testament: A New Translation (Joseph Bryant Rotherham), Kregel Publications.

[11] The New Testament of our Lord and Savior Jesus Christ, American Bible Union Version (John A. Broadus), United Bible Society.

- restrict

God put His boundaries around His Holy Day, the Sabbath, (Saturday), His day to do the things that please Him the most and not us.

God had to remind David about His Holy Day, saying HEAR MY VOICE and don't harden your heart.

Notice: Today, after so long a time;

In the beginning, of time, when God created the heavens and the earth, it was about 4000B.C. at the time Adam was formed. God Rested and sanctify the seventh day of the week. Genesis 2:2, 3

Then in the year of 1498 B.C. Moses brought the children of Israel to Mount Sinai where God spoke to all of Israel and wrote His commandments on tables of stone. In which He declares His Holy Sabbath Rest, along with the rest of His commandments,

Then after such a long time David is born around the year 1085 B.C. and is anointed in the year 1065 B.C. David lives to be 70 years old. During this time of David's life God reminds David about His Holy Sabbath, in turn King David reminds the people to listen to God and not harden their hearts.

After about 433 years from the giving of the torah to Moses and the children of Israel, God must remind the people of the covenant through David.

Today we must be reminded yet still of His Holy Day and the covenant.

Just as stated in Exodus 20:8, *Remember the Sabbath Day, to keep it Holy.*

> *For if Jesus had given them rest, then would he not afterward spoken of another day* (v. 8).
>
> *For if Joshua had given them rest* (ASV).
>
> *For if Joshua had really brought them rest* (GSPD[12]).

---

[12] The New Testament: An American Translation (Edgar Goodspeed), copyright 1923, 1948 by the University of Chicago Press).

...not concerning another he would have spoken after these things day (Greek Inter).

If God really gave Israel Rest then He would have told us about another day, but has not.

There remaineth therefore a rest to the people of God (v. 9).

So there must still be a promised Sabbath rest for God's people (GSPD).

There still exist, therefore a full and complete rest for the people of God (PHI).

There remains therefore a Sabbath rest for the people of God (ASV).

For he that is entered into his rest, he also hath ceased from his own works, as God did from his (v. 10).

Let us labor therefore to enter into his rest, lest any man fall after the same example of unbelief (v. 11).

Let us therefore give diligence to enter that no man fall after the same example of disobedience (ASV).

Let us therefore earnestly strive to enter (ALF[13]).

Let us therefore make every effort to enter so that none of us falls through such disbelief as that of which we have an example (TCNT).

Let us be eager to know this rest for ourselves (PHI).

...into the same sort of disobedience (MOF).

What I get out of this chapter is the writer is talking about a certain day that God has set up, a day God sanctified in Genesis 2:2-3.

Ok, how do we go about laboring to enter into God's Rest?

Thus saith the Lord, Stand ye in the ways, and see, and ask for the old paths where is the good way, and walk

---

13 The New Testament (Henry Alford).

> *therein, and ye shall find rest for your souls* (Jeremiah 6:16).

What are the old paths? The old paths are the same path that he told Abraham, Isaac, and Jacob.

> *O ye seed of Israel his servant, ye children of Jacob, his chosen ones.*
>
> *He is the Lord our God; his judgments are in all the earth.*
>
> *Be mindful always of his covenant; the word which he commanded to a thousand generations; even of the covenant which he made with Abraham, and his oath unto Isaac;*
>
> *and hath confirmed the same to Jacob for a law, and to Israel for an everlasting covenant* (1 Chronicles 16:13-17).

These are the old paths, when we follow the old path we will live.

> *Ye shall do my judgments, and keep mine ordinances, to walk therein: I am the Lord your God.*
>
> *Ye shall therefore keep my statutes, and my judgments: which if a man do, he shall live in them: I am the Lord* (Leviticus 18:4-5).

The Lord tells us in Matthew 11 also how to find Rest for our souls.

> *Come unto me all ye that labor and are heavy laden, and I will give you rest.*
>
> *Take my yoke upon you and learn of me; for I am meek and lowly in heart: and ye shall find rest unto your souls* (Matthew 11:28-29).

Let's look at this verse and see just what the Lord is talking about.

Who are the heavy-laden? These are people that are burdened and oppressed down with sorrow and sin. He is telling us to come to him to find Rest.

But, what is it that He is telling us to do? Take His Yoke. What is Jesus Yoke?

Yoke = in Greek – zeugnumi

- a mark or sign of slavery or subjection
- bondage...servitude
- a bond or tie of marriage
- a law or obligation
- to be intimate companions

Thus when we take up His yoke, we take up His laws and ways that He has set down for us to follow. Thus, we become His bondservant or a servant to His will and His Fathers. Because Jesus told us to do the Father's will as He also has done His Father's will.

When we come to know God and become His servants, we also become a free will servant to the King. What the King says goes. Long live the King.

The King set forth His covenant in the beginning and signed it in blood. As He tells us in Jeremiah 6:16 to stand in the way and look for the old paths. Where do we find the paths, in the covenant given in the beginning?

> *And he took the book of the covenant, and read in the audience of the people: and they said, All the Lord hath said will we do and be obedient.*
>
> *And Moses took the blood, and sprinkled it on the people, and said, Behold the blood of the covenant, which the Lord hath made with you concerning all these words* (Exodus 24:7-8).

This is when we will find Rest for our souls. Now and in the new heaven and earth, when we follow the King.

THE REASON FOR THE REST

In six days God created the heaven and the earth, and on the seventh day He Rested and was refreshed. Then he blessed it and sanctified the seventh day.

In Leviticus, the Lord says, *six days shall work be done: but on the seventh day is the Sabbath of Rest, a holy convocation; ye shall do no work therein: it is the Sabbath of the Lord in all your dwellings* (Leviticus 23:3).

God tells us that we can do anything that we want far as work, play, and worship for six days, but on the seventh day, it is a holy convocation, (rehearsal). Each week we would rehearse, by resting from our labors and hearing the word of the Lord. By rehearsing we are telling the story of the day of the Lord. How is that?

This is how; each day is equal to a thousand years.

> *But, beloved, be not ignorant of this one thing, that one day is with the Lord as a thousand years, and a thousand years as a day* (2 Peter 3:8).
>
> *But the day of the Lord will come* (2 Peter 3:10).
>
> *For a thousand years, in thy sight are but yesterday when it past, and as a watch in the night* (Psalms 90:4).

Each week when we rehearse, we are rehearsing the day of the Lord.

Thus far we have come 6000 years in history. From Adam to the coming of the Christ the first time is 4 days or 4000 years. And from Christ hanging on the tree to now is 2 days or 2000 years. The next day is the day of the Lord, which will last for a thousand years, the Sabbath rest of God, Thus we have the 7th day or 7000 years.

Revelation 20 tells about, the thousand years, during this time the Devil the wicked one will be bound so he will not deceive anyone, until the end of the thousand years.

If we do not participate in keeping of God's Rest the seventh day Sabbath now, by rehearsing it each week, then we may not be entering into the true rest either.

We will be counted along with those that died in the wilderness. The second wilderness is the second death for those that do not believe.

Let us labor therefore to enter into His Rest, lest any man fall after the same example of unbelief.

The Lord says, *"They do always err in their heart; and they have not known my ways. So I swear in my wrath, they shall not enter into my rest"* (Hebrews 3:10).

THE HOLIDAYS

Ah the holidays, we all love the holidays. The warm fuzzes, the get together with family and friends, a time in which we don't go to work. Most everything shuts down and comes to a stand still for about 12 to 24 hours, no hustle and bustle, and a time to be quite and relax.

Did you know that God has given us all kind of holidays or holy days? These are the feasts and festivals. Leviticus 23 lists many of the feasts. One of the feasts is the weekly Sabbath Rest. We shut down all the worldly actives we have going on and get together with family and friends and feast together on the word of the Lord, and break bread together.

We have other major feast and festival that we get to do, which God has put in place for us to do. These are for all generations. Each nation has their own holidays, which we institute for different reasons, just like God instituted His Holy Days and His feast and festival. Here is a list of His Holy convocations. These feasts and festival tell His story of how He will redeem His people and how He will dwell with man in the new heaven and earth. When we participate in these feasts and festival we get a better understanding of God's wonderful plan that He set forth from the foundation of the earth.

- Feast of unleavened Bread--Passover-- Aviv 15-21--March, April
- First fruits--Aviv 22--March, April
- Feast of Shavot--Pentecost--Siwan--6-12--May, June
- Rosh HaShana- Trumpets- Tishri 1-9--Sept., Oct
- Yom Kippur-- Day of Atonement-- Tishri -10-- Sept, Oct

- Feast of Sukkot--Tabernacles-- Tishri -15-22--Sept., Oct
- Festival of Hanukkah-- Dedication of Lights--Kislew 25-Teveth 2-Nov., Dec
- Purim-- Adar 14-15--Feb.
- Weekly Sabbath

What is a feast and a festival?

FEAST:

1. a periodical celebration, or day or time of celebration, of religious or other character, in commemoration of some event or person, or having some special significance.
2. a sumptuous entertainment or meal for many guests.
3. any rich or abundant meal
4. to dwell with gratification or delight

FESTIVAL:

1. a periodic religious or other feast
2. an anniversary for festive celebration
3. pertaining to a feast or holiday

Which Holidays do you keep? Men or God's.

THE MACCABEES

Testimony from the pages of the Maccabee, Written in the year 134-104 B.C.

During the time of Alexander the great and the reign of Antiochus Epiphanes. This is the History of some of the things that took place to the people of God, and what happen to them.

> *"In those days lawless people came forth from Israel, and misled many, saying, Let us go and make covenant with the Gentiles round about us, for since* ***we separated from them*** *many evils have come upon us.*
>
> *This proposal pleased them, and some of the people eagerly went to the king. He authorized them to observe the ordinances of the Gentiles. So the built a gymnasium in Jerusalem. According to the Gentile custom, and removed the marks of circumcision, and* ***abandoned the holy covenant****.*
>
> *They joined with the Gentiles and sold themselves to do evil"* (1 Maccabees1:12-14).
>
> *"When Antiochus saw that his kingdom was established, he determine to become king of the land"* (1:17).
>
> *"Then the king wrote to his whole kingdom that all should be one people, and that each should give up his customs. All the Gentiles accepted the command of the king. Many even from Israel gladly adopted his religion"* (1:43-44).
>
> *"they sacrificed to idols and* ***profaned the Sabbath****. And the king sent letters by messengers to Jerusalem and the cities of Judah; he directed them to follow the customs strange to the land, to forbid burnt offerings and*

> *sacrifices and drink offerings in the sanctuary,* ***to profane the Sabbath and feast****, to defile the sanctuary and priest, to build altars and sacred precincts and shrines for idols, to sacrifice swine and unclean animals, and to leave their sons uncircumcised"* (1:45-47).

> *"They were to make themselves abominable by everything unclean and profane,* ***so that they should forget the law and change all of the ordinances****. And whoever does not obey the command of the king shall die"* (1:48).

> *"Many of the people, everyone who forsook the law, joined them, and they did evil in the land, they drove Israel into hiding in every place of refuge they had"* (1:55).

> *"The books of the law, which they found, they tore to pieces and burned with fire. Where the book of the covenant was found in the possession of anyone, or if any one adhered to the law, the decree of the king condemned him to death"* (1:59-60).

> *"But many in Israel stood firm and were resolved in their hearts not to eat unclean food. They chose to die rather than to be defiled by food or to* ***profane the holy covenant****; and they did die. And very great wrath came upon Israel"* (1:65).

There will always be a remnant of people on the earth that will always do things God's way no matter what the cost, Even though many will depart from the faith.

There were a few, that made that decision in this time period. Let's see what Mattathias says:

> *"But Mattathias answered and said in a loud voice: Even if all the nations that live under the rule of the king obey him, and have chosen to do his commandments, departing each one from the religion of his fathers,* ***yet I and my son and my brothers will live by the covenant*** *of our fathers* (1 Maccabees 2:19).

Far be it from us to desert the law and the ordinances. We will not obey the king's words by turning aside from our religion to the right hand or to the left (v. 22).

When he was finished speaking these words, a Jew came forward in the sight of all to offer sacrifice upon the altar in Modein, according to the king's command. When Mattathias saw it, he burned with zeal and his heart was stirred. He gave vent to his righteous anger; he ran and killed him upon the altar. At the same time he killed the king's officer who was forcing them to sacrifice, and tore down the altar....Then Mattathias cried out in the city with a loud voice, saying: Let everyone who is zealous for the law and supports the covenant come out with me" (2:23-25)*!!*

"Then there was another man that rose up his name was Maccabeeus. He was the son of Judas.

He, Maccabeeus, extended the glory of his people. Like a giant he put on his breastplate; he girded on his armor of war and waged battles, protecting the host by his sword. He was like a lion in his deeds, like a lion's cub roaring for prey. He searched out and pursued the lawless; he burned those who trouble his people. Lawless men shrank back for fear of him; and evildoers were confounded; and deliverance prospered by his hand" (1 Maccabees 3:1-5).

No matter how many or few that there is, if you stand in the way of the Lord, He will deliver his people.

"But when they saw the army coming to meet them, they said to Judas, How can we, few as we are, fight against so great and strong a multitude? And we are faint for we have eaten nothing today. Judas replied; it is easy for many to be hemmed in by a few, for in the sight of Heaven there is no difference between saving by many or by few. It is not the size of the army that the victory in battle depends, but strength comes from Heaven" (3:17).

"Thus, they fought; they fought for their lives and for the Laws of the most High God. So the Lord fought before

> *them and crushed the armies before them. And fear fell on upon all the Gentiles around about them"* (3:21).

To know more about what happens in the history of the Maccabees, read the book of 1 Maccabees. (Maccabees from the Oxford Annotated Bible with apocrypha.)

No matter who we are if we stand in the ways of God, His laws and ordinances, we belong to God, let's walk in His ways, then He will fight for us through many ways.

Will we be part of the remnant of God, look at what Revelation 12:17 says happens to the remnant.

> *And the dragon was wroth with the woman, and went to make war with the remnant of her seed, which keep the commandments of God, and have the testimony of Jesus Christ.*

Where will we stand? In the remnant or outside the remnant?

THE CHANGES

Things change; at least that's what people say. As we go through time everything changes. To a point it does. People are born and people die. We move here and then there. We make new friends and miss old friends. Man is constantly changing the face of the earth, either making it better or making it worst. Depending on how we look at it. But with all this History repeats itself. In Ecclesiastes, Solomon says that there is nothing new under the sun. It may be new to us but not to our forefathers.

But what about God, does He change or change His will?

> *For I am the Lord, **I change not**; therefore ye sons of Jacob are not consumed. Even from the days of your fathers ye are gone away from mine ordinances, and have not kept them. Return to me, and I will return unto you, saith the Lord of hosts* (Malachi 3:6-7).
>
> ***Every word of God is PURE**: he is a shield to them that put their trust in him. Add thou not unto his words, lest he reprove thee, and thou be found **a liar*** (Proverbs 30:5-6).
>
> *He that saith, I know him, and keepeth not his commandments, **is a liar**, and the truth is not in him* (1 John 2:4).
>
> *My covenant will I not break, nor alter the thing that is gone out of my lips* (Psalms 89:34).
>
> *...all his commandments are sure. They stand fast for ever and ever* (Psalms 111:7-8).

We see that God does not change nor does His word. Jesus says that man cannot live by bread alone. But every word that proceeds out of the mouth of God.

But, what does He tell us to do?

> *Ye shall not add unto the word, which I command you; neither shall ye diminish aught from it, that ye may keep the commandments of the Lord your God, which I command you* (Deuteronomy 4:2).
>
> *What thing soever I command you, observe to do it: thou shalt not add thereto nor diminish from it* (Deuteronomy 12:32).

Notice that these passages are from the torah. The Old Testament, where God breathes the word or spoke the word to Moses His servant which he tells the people.

> *For I testify unto every man that heareth the words of the prophecy of this book, If any man shall add unto these things, God shall add unto him the plagues that are written in this book: And if any man shall take away from the words of the book of this prophecy, God shall take his part out of the book of life, and out of the holy city, and from the things, which are written in this book* (Revelation 22:18-19).

Before the day of wrath or the second coming of the Lord, He tells His people to do something and that is to remember something.

What's that?

> *Remember ye the* ***Law of Moses*** *my servant, which I commanded unto him in Horeb for all of Israel, with statutes and judgments* (Malachi 4:4).

So God is telling us to remember and to do His ways, but what is it that we are always doing?

We the inhabitants of the earth change the laws of God to our ways, but in the end to no avail to us.

> *And he shall speak great words against the most high, and shall wear out the saints of the most High, and* ***to think to change times and laws****: and they shall be given into his hand (*Daniel 7:25).

This will apply to anyone of us that think that we can improve on God's laws and statutes. Thus we become part of the beast system and not even know it.

What does God say about the earth and the people that dwell on the earth?

> *The earth is defiled under the inhabitants thereof; because they (we) have transgressed the laws, changed the ordinance, broken the everlasting covenant* (Isaiah 24:5).

What we the inhabitants of the earth need to do is to go back to the old paths of our father Abraham, Isaac, and Jacob. Jesus said to do the Father's will as He has done.

WHO CHANGED WHAT

Ok, So we see that God does not change nor does His word. But then who did the changing?

> *Isaiah says,* ***the inhabitants of the earth****.... Who are the inhabitants of the earth?* ***We are****, both Jew and Gentile that are alive on the earth, and our children after us* (Isaiah 24:5).

As we look a little closer, we will find that the leaders of the both the political and religious areas are the ones that seem to have the power to bring about these changes. And the rest of us seem to follow along without challenging the powers that be. Then the preachers and teachers in turn promote these changes. Some knowingly and others of us unknowingly, because we have not really studied the true word and tried the spirits. As we have seen in Deuteronomy 13: 1-4 God says that if we harken unto these prophets and are turned away to other god's, then it is to prove us or test us to see if we are true to Him. (God)

Now, Let us look at some of the people that made these changes throughout our history.

1. In around 134-104 B.C we see that Antiochus Epiphanies caused the people of God to abandon the holy covenant and profane the Sabbath.[14]
2. In 117 A.D. Emperor Hadrain issued an imperial edict forbidding religious practices of the Jews such as circumcision, observance of the Sabbath, and public reading of the law.[15]

---

[14] Maccabees to see the whole story read the Maccabees

[15] History of the Christian Church, 1933, Lars P. Qualben, p 72.

3. Constantine himself continued to hold the traditional office of " pontifex maximus" or high priest for the official pagan worship.[16]

   In 321 A.D. He gave the Catholic but not the heretical churches the right to receive legacies.

   In 321 A.D. He enjoined the civil observances of Sunday.[17] Edict of March 7,321 A.D. "Let all the judges and town people, and the occupation of all trades rest on the venerable day of the sun."(venerabili die solis) Corpus Juris Civilis Cod., lib.3, tit12, lex.3 /enc.britannica, 9 edition
4. In 364 A.D. The Catholic Church, in the council of Laodicea transferred the solemnity from Saturday to Sunday.[18]
5. The Catholic Church mark of authority. "Sunday is our mark of authority... the church is above the Bible, and this transference of Sabbath observance is proof of that fact."[19]
6. "Sunday is a Catholic institution and its claim to observance can be defended only on Catholic principles.... From beginning to end of scripture there is not a single passage that warrants the transfer of weekly public worship from the last day of the week to the first"[20]
7. Question. How prove you that the Church hath power to command feast and holy days?

   Answer: "By the very act of changing the Sabbath into Sunday, which Protestants allow, and therefore they fondly contradict themselves, by keeping Sunday strictly, and breaking most other feasts commanded by the same Church."[21]

---

[16] Ibid, p.99.

[17] Ibid, 117.

[18] The Convert's Catechism of Catholic Doctrine, p 50, 3 Edition.

[19] The Catholic Record, London Ontario, Sept.1, 1923

[20] Catholic press. Sydney, Australia, August 1900, that has changed the instructions and statutes and judgments of God, and then we are then following after the beast. Who is the beast?

[21] James Cardinal Gibbons, Archbishop of Baltimore (1877-1921)

As we can see in these seven examples that people were in great position of power have instituted the changes from the way God set up for us to follow.

So many of us just play follow the leader. So when we play follow the leader of any one I say the father of the beast. It is no more than the Devil, Satan, the father of lies himself. We follow after the beast, because his ministers pervert the True Word of God to lead us away after other gods.

Many may say ignorance is bliss. Well, is ignorance really bliss, in some cases it may be. But when it comes to the Word of God.

> *For they, being ignorant of God's righteousness and going about to establish their own righteousness, and have not submitted themselves unto the righteousness of God* (Romans10:3).

> *And the times of this ignorance God winked at; but now commandeth all men every where to repent* (Acts 17:30).

> *This I say therefore, and testify in the Lord, that ye henceforth walk not as other Gentiles walk, in the vanity of their mind. Having the understanding darkened, being alienated from the life of God through the ignorance that is in them, because of the blindness of their heart* (Ephesians 4:17-18).

> *His (Satan's) watchmen are blind: they are all ignorant, they are all dumb as dogs, they can not bark; sleeping, lying down, and loving to slumber. Yea, they are greedy dogs, which can never have enough, and they are shepherds that cannot understand: they all look to their own way, everyone for his gain, from his quarter* (Isaiah 56:10).

> *They be blind leaders of the blind, and if the blind lead the blind, both shall fall into the ditch (pit, lake of fire)* (Matthew 15:14).

When we find out that we have been following down the wrong path let us repent and turn toward the Lord God. We need to come to the true knowledge of the Lord. The Lord says that his people perish for the lack of knowledge.

Many of us have very small amount of true knowledge, because we are drawn away by the other things and amusements in life that we don't spend the time in the word. We let someone else, spend time in the word, while we enjoy the pleasures of this life.

Matthew 6:32, 33 tells us to seek after the kingdom of God and not after the things that the Gentiles seek. Many of the Gentiles have come to know the Lord and are still seeking after the things of this world. Where your treasure is so is your hearts. Is our hearts in the things of God or the things of the world, *I think I will tear down this barn, (house) and build a bigger barn, (house) a better car, etc, and then tomorrow we die.*

This is the case with us today. We have one building; we either sell it or tear it down and build a bigger one. Many times to please our own egos to say look at me. And yet we are so far in debt that we work three jobs to keep up with it.

And Yet the Lord said, owe no man anything, but we owe all men all kinds of things. So who is in bondage and who are we in bondage to?

Is it not to this world system by the leaders that enslave us with debt, by which it is hard to get out? Thus not having the freedom that we should have.

Is it not Satan, which is the Slave Master, which wants to make slaves of all of us through with his many devices?

CHURCH LEADERS SPEAK OUT

Let us turn and look at what some of the church leaders through time have said about the change, or lack of change about the Rest of God, the Sabbath Saturday, the seventh day of the week.

1. Isaac Williams.... "And where are we told in the scriptures that we are to keep the first day at all? We are commanded to keep the seventh; but we are nowhere commanded to keep the first day..."[22]

2. Bishop Seymour..." We have made the change from the seventh day to the first day, from Saturday to Sunday, on the authority of the holy Catholic Church"[23]

3. Dr. R.W. Dale.... "It is quite clear that however rigidly or devotedly we may spend Sunday, we are not keeping the Sabbath...The Sabbath was founded on a specific Divine command. We can plead no such command for the obligation to observe Sunday."[24]

4. Alexander Campbell...." But say some, it was changed from the seventh to the first day. Where? When? And by whom? No man can tell. NO; it never changed, nor could it be, unless creation was to be gone through again; for the reason assigned must be changed before the observance, or respect to the reason, can be changed! It is all old wives fables to talk of the change of the Sabbath from the seventh to the first day. If it changed, it was that august personage changed it who changes times and laws ex officio- I think his name is Doctor Antichrist"[25]

---

[22] Plain Sermons on the Catechism, Vol. 1, pp 334, 336

[23] Bishop Seymour, Why We Keep Sunday.

[24] Dr. R. W. Dale, *The Ten Commandments*, New York, Eaton & Mains p. 127-129.

5. Lutheran..." We have seen how gradually the impression of the Jewish Sabbath faded from the mind of the Christian Church, and how completely the newer though underlying the observance of the first day took possession of the Church. WE have seen Christian for the first three centuries never confused one with the other."[26]

6. D.L. Moody..."The Sabbath was binding in Eden, and it has been in force ever since. The fourth commandment begins with the word remember, showing that the Sabbath already existed when God wrote the laws on the tables of stone at Sinai. How can men claim that this one commandment has been done away with when they will admit that the other nine are still binding?"[27]

7. Lipscomb and Sewell.... "The first day of the week is not the Sabbath day in any sense. It is unscriptural and untrue to call it such, the whole denominational world is in error on this subject...." "The Sabbath never was changed from the seventh to the first day of the week. The seventh day was the only Sabbath. The Sabbath Law and the scripture on the first day of the week do not have any connection with each other..."[28]

8. T.C. Black, D.D...."The Sabbath is part of the Decalogue-the ten commandments. This alone forever settles the question as to the perpetuity of the institution. Until, therefore, it can be shown that the whole Moral Law has been repealed, the Sabbath will stand.... The teaching of Christ confirms the perpetuity of the Sabbath."[29]

9. Regarding the change from the observance of the Jewish Sabbath to the Christian Sunday, I wish to draw you attention to the facts:

a. That Protestants, who accept the Bible as the only rule of faith and religion, should by all means go back to the observance of the Sabbath, The fact that they do not, but

---

[25] Alexander Campbell, *The Christian Baptist*, Feb.2, 1824, Vol.1, No 7, p 164.

[26] The Sunday Problem, A Study Book of the United Lutheran Church, (1923), p.36.

[27] D. L. Moody, *Weighed and Wanting*, pp.7, 48.

[28] Lipscomb and Sewell, *Question and Answers*, 1921, p574, 577.

[29] T. C. Black, D.D., *Theology Condensed*, pp.474, Presbyterian.

on the contrary observe the Sunday, stultifies them in the eyes of every thinking man.

b. We Catholics do not accept the Bible as the only rule of faith. Besides the Bible we have the living Church, the authority of the Church, as a rule to guide us. We say, this Church instituted by Christ to teach and guide man through life, has the right to change the ceremonial laws of the Old Testament and hence, we accept her change of the Sabbath to Sunday. We frankly say, yes, the Church made this change made this Law; she made many other laws, for instance, the Friday abstinence, the unmarried priesthood, the laws concerning mixed marriages, the regulation of Catholic marriages and a thousand other laws.

It is always somewhat laughable; to see Protestant churches, in pulpit and legislation, demand the observance of Sunday, of which there is nothing in their Bible."[30]

As we can see that many of the old time leaders of the different Churches show that God has not changed His word, but Man has made the changes.

> *For laying aside the commandment of God, ye hold the tradition of men, as the washing of pots and cups: and many others such like things ye do. And he said unto them, Full well ye reject the commandment of God, that ye many keep your own tradition* (Mark 7:8-9).
>
> *Wherefore if ye were dead with Christ from the rudiments of the world, why, as though living in the world, are ye subject to ordinances, Which all are to perish with using: after the commandments and doctrine of men* (Colossians 2:20, 22)*?*
>
> *...but in vain they do worship me, teaching for doctrines the commandments of men* (Matthew 15:9).

---

[30] Peter R. Kraemer, Catholic Church Extension Society (1975) Chicago, IL.

Are we ready to return to the way of the Lord, in keeping His statutes and commandments? Or do we want to continue in our own vain thinking?

What is your choice?

THE LANGUAGES

> *And the whole earth was of one language and of one speech.* (Genesis 11:1).
>
> *Go to, let us go down, and there confound their language, that they may not understand one another's speech* (Genesis 11:7).

Languages the way people talk to each other. No matter how you say it God's Holy Day is still the same.

At Mount Sinai there were around 70 languages or dialects that the people spoke in. Now there is way over 11,000 languages or dialects used to communicate with each other. Now we have the computer, which will translate the language for us with the right program. Even the computer has its own language. We have to learn it to be able to communicate with the other people of different languages.

How many languages can you say Sabbath in?

These are just a few of the many languages.

God made sure that we knew and know what day is His day throughout time.

English - Seventh Day- Sabbath	Hebrew -yom hash-shab-bath
England English- Saturday	shemitic - yom hash-abo-vi-i
Hebrew modern -shab-bath	Ancient Syriac- shab-ba-tho
Assyrian - sa-ba-tu	Baylonian - sa-ba-tu
Ethiopic - san-bat	Falasha - yini sanbat
Hindustani - shamba	Armenian - shapat

Chinese (R.C.) - chan li t si

Khassi - ka angi sait jain

Malayan - hari sabtu

Russian - subbota

Swedish - lordag

Polish - sobota

Prussian - sabatico

Latin - sabbatum

Annamite - ngay thu bay

Tibetan - za pen pa

Malagassy - alsabotsy

Icelandic - laugardagur

Danish - laverdag

High German - samstag

Spanish - sabado

Italian - sabbato

BUT, BUT, WHAT ABOUT

But, we have always gone to church on Sundays for many generations?

It doesn't matter what our parents or grandparents have done in the past, what matters, is what we will do now when we are beginning to understand God's Holy Day that he wants us to keep. We can go to church 7 days a week if we want. But what God wants to know is how, will we keep His day Holy. He gave us the other 6 to do whatever we want when it comes to work, play or worship.

But, what am I going to do about work. I work every Saturday?

To start with you need to pray to God about this so He provides you a way to get a new job or that things will work out with the job that you are on now.

We need to start working this out. The word says "*to work out our* ***salvation with fear and trembling****....*" Phil.2:12. Be ready to know what the consequences may be when you get ready to take a stand for what you now know to be true.

To tell, about a case at hand. One job that I was working at I worked every weekend. Then I began to learn about the true Sabbath of God. At first I would talk to people like I already understood even though I did not completely, as I began to understand more things began to work out. I tried to get Sundays off to go to church and that did not happen. So I waited a little while, then I requested off on Saturdays not giving any real reason at the time I got Saturday's off. Then one of the men that I worked with went on vacation so I worked those two Saturday's that he was on vacation, When he came back I did not work anymore.

After several months later I received a new job with every weekend off.

Be patient, trust in the Lord and He will work it out for you, provided that your Heart is right with God. If it's not it may not work out or you are being tested on your faith.

But I have a retail business that is open 7 days a week?

Anyone that has a retail business has the power to open and close when they want. When we come to grips with the facts what God wants and close our business on His day even though the rest of the world will be open for the almighty buck. We will then find that God may test you for a while. You will be looking at business dropping off and want to open back up. But if you prove faithful to God then God will in turn begin to bless your business, because you are in the process of pleasing Him on His Holy Day.

This then becomes a test of Faith.

What about GRACE, I thought that we were under grace and not Law?

What about grace? What is grace; it is favor, mercy, and acceptance, to start. Many of us have a misconception of what grace is and when it started.

We use the passage: *For by grace are ye saved through faith; and that not of your selves: it is the gift of God: Not of works, lest any man should boast* (Ephesians 2:8-9).

Many of us think that grace came after Jesus came to earth in the form of man. He is grace and truth.

> *And the Word was made flesh, and dwelt among us, (and we beheld his glory, the glory of the only begotten of the Father), full of grace and truth. John bare witness of him, and cried, saying, this was he whom I spoke, he that cometh after me is preferred before me: for he was before me. And of his fulness have all we received, and grace for grace. For the law, was given by Moses, but grace and truth came by Jesus Christ* (John. 1:14-16).

God was in the beginning of time before the foundation of the earth, and he made all things that were made.

He is the one that gave the laws to Moses to write down on paper so the people would know what his will is. The forefathers knew what the will of the Father was in the beginning. So let us go to the beginning of time and look at some people. First we will look at Noah found in Genesis 6:8, 9.

> ***But Noah found grace in the eyes of the Lord.***
>
> *Noah was a just man and perfect in his generations, and Noah walked with God.*

Here we see that God told a man to build an ark because the world was very wicked. Yet out of the whole world at the time there was just one man that found grace or favor in the eyes of the Lord.

Why was this? How did He, Noah find favor with God?

Let's consider some things first.

1. What was the Law given for or should I say written down for?

> *The law was given because of transgressions* (Galatians 3:19).

For the world to be wicked at this time there was some form of instructions, commandments, statutes or judgments that were to be followed. If there were not then there would be no sin.

2. What is SIN?

> *Whosoever committeth sin transgresseth also the law: for sin is the transgression of the law* (1 John 3:4).

3. The law is to show us our sins.

> *What shall we say then? Is the law sin? God forbid. Nay, I had not known sin, but by the law: for I had not known lust, except the law had said, Thou shalt not covet.*
>
> *But sin taking occasion by the commandment, wrought in me all manner of concupiscence. For without the law sin was dead.*

> *For I was alive without the law once: but when the commandment came, sin revived, and I died.*
>
> *And the commandment, which was ordained to life, I found to be unto death.*
>
> *For sin taking occasion by the commandment, deceived me, and by it slew me.*
>
> *Wherefore the law is holy and the commandment holy, and just and good* (Romans 7:7-12).

So how did Noah find grace in the eyes of the Lord?

Noah knew what the will of the father was, because he knew what the commandments of God were to follow. So Noah walked according to the commandments of God. He walked upright in the sight of God.

> *For the Lord God is a sun and shield: The Lord will give grace and glory: no good thing will he withhold from them that walk uprightly* (Psalms 84:11).

Noah was a JUST man. What is a Just man? Strong's– H6662– righteous, lawful.

> *The just shall live by faith* (Romans 1:17).
>
> *For not the hearers of the law are just before God but the doers of the law shall be justified* (Righteous) (Romans 2:13).
>
> *For ye have need of patience, that after ye have done the will of God, ye might receive the promise. For yet a little while, and he that shall come will come, and will not tarry. Now the Just shall live by faith: but if any man draws back, my soul shall have no pleasure in him* (Hebrews 10:36-38).

Noah was perfect.

Strong's H8549, complete, truth, integrity, sound, upright, full,

G5046, growth mental and moral character, completeness

> *Be ye therefore perfect, even as your Father, which is heaven, is perfect* (Matthew 5:48).
>
> *The disciple is not above his Master: but every one that is perfect shall be as his master* (Luke 6:40).
>
> *Mark the perfect man, and behold the upright: for the end of that man is peace* (Psalms 37:37).
>
> .... *that ye may stand perfect and complete in all of the will of God* (Colossians 4:12).

Noah walked by faith in that he believed what God gave him instructions to do. Thus he did the will of God to a point that he was without spot before God. And became as God was.

Let's back up to Enoch, Genesis 5:23,24

> *And Enoch lived sixty and five years, and begat Methuselah:*
>
> *And Enoch walked with God after he begat Methuselah three hundred years, and begat sons and daughters:*
>
> *And all the days of Enoch were three hundred sixty and five years:*
>
> *And Enoch walked with God: and he was not: for God took him.*
>
> *Enoch was taught the will of God from his birth up. He walked in the instructions of God, because He was taught them from his parents. He continued in them all through Life.*
>
> *Enoch was 65 when He had his firstborn. He continue to walk uprightly with God for another 300 years.*

Enoch bore the testimony that pleased God all the days of his life.

> *By Faith Enoch was translated that he should not see death; and was not found, because God had translated him: for before his translation he had the testimony, which please God* (Hebrews 11:5).

Enoch walked in the lifestyle that God had been requiring people to live. Enoch's testimony bore witness of God and His word. Thus finding grace (favor) in God's eyes.

Abraham

> *And when Abram was ninety years old and nine, the Lord appeared to Abram and said unto him, I am the Almighty God: walk before me and be thou perfect. And I will make my covenant between thee, and me and I will multiply thee exceedingly* (Genesis 17:1-2).

As we have seen that when you walk before God, these were upright and full of the Lord in keeping his word. Abram was complete and in truth with the Lord.

> *Abraham believed God and it was counted unto him for righteousness* (Romans 4:3).

Moses

> *Now therefore, I pray thee, if I have found grace in thy sight, show me now thy way, that I may know thee, that I may find grace in thy sight:*
>
> *For wherein shall it be known here that thy people and I have found grace in thy sight? Is it not that thou goest with us?*
>
> *And the Lord said to Moses, I will do this thing also that thou hast spoken: for thou hast found grace in my sight* (Exodus 33:13,16-17).

How do we find grace in God's sight as Moses asked: to be shown the way of the Lord, thus we find favor from the Lord and end up knowing the Lord?

> *And hereby do we know that we know him, if we keep his commandments. He that saith, I know him, and keepeth not his commandments, is a liar, and the truth is not in him. But whoso keepeth his word, in him verily is the love of God perfected* (1 John 1:3-5).

> *And whatsoever we ask, we receive of him, because we keep his commandments, and do those things that are pleasing in his sight* (1 John 3:22).

Grace faith and law go hand in hand. To receive God's grace we have the faith to do the things contained in the law, thus walking upright before God and then finding favor in God's eyes, thus becoming just or righteous before God.

The Law shows us the way of God and how He wants us to live. Then we need enough Faith to really believe God and do the things that He has instructed for us to do. When we do this we begin to walk in the spirit and not the flesh.

> *There fore there is no condemnation to them, which are in Christ Jesus, who walk not after the flesh, but after the spirit* (Rom.8:1).

So if Christ makes us free, should we sin?

> *What shall we say then? Shall we continue in sin, that grace may abound? God forbid. How shall we that are dead to sin, live any longer therein* (Romans 6:1-2)*?*

What is sin? Sin is the transgression of the Law of God.

> *What shall we say then? Is the law sin? God forbid. Nay, I had not known sin, but by the law: for I had not known lust, except the law had said, Thou shalt not covet* (Romans 7:7).

So, when we walk in the spirit according to the commandments of God we begin to walk upright in God's eyes finding Grace or favor in the eyes of God through the son of God. But as we walk according to the flesh we begin to lose favor in the eyes of God and he will turn his face from us until we repent. If unrepented as we see in Galatians 5:19-22. When we continue to walk in the flesh then we will not inherit the kingdom of God. So the works of the flesh were determined by God in the instructions that He gave to the people through Moses and before, because God destroyed a whole race of people but eight, Noah and his family.

But the law wasn't it done away with?

The cry comes out from many of us that we are not under the law. It was done away with.

What law was done away with? There are many laws or instruction that God set down in His Holy Word.

What is Law any way? What does the Law really refer to?

To find out we will go to the Strong's Concordance and find out what it says that law is.

Strong's – number for LAW is: H8451 – torah

- precept
- statue
- Decalogue
- Pentateuch
- royal edict
- commandment
- decree
- commission

This is the first five books in the Bible. The Kings James Version calls this:

- the law, Deuteronomy 4:4
- law of Moses, Joshua 8:31
- law of God, Nehemiah 8:8
- law of the Lord their God, Nehemiah 9:3
- the covenant, Exodus 24:7

In Nehemiah,

> *Also day by day, from the first day unto the last day, he read in the book of the law (torah) of God* (Nehemiah 8:18).

When God spoke to the people and Moses this is what He gave them.

> *Thou camest down also upon the Mount Sinai, and spakest with them from heaven, and gavest them right judgments, and true laws, good statutes and commandments:*
>
> *And makest known unto them thy holy Sabbath, and commandedest them precepts, statutes, and laws, (torah) by the hand of Moses thy servant* (Nehemiah 9:13-14).

This is what the Lord says:

> *Think not that I am come to destroy the law (torah) or the prophets: I am not come to destroy, but fulfill.*
>
> *For verily I say unto you, till heaven and earth pass, one jot or one tittle shall in no wise pass from the law (torah), till all be fulfilled.*
>
> *Whosoever therefore shall break one of these commandments, and shall teach men so he shall be called the least in the kingdom of heaven: but whatsoever shall do and teach them, the same shall be called great in the kingdom of heaven.*
>
> *For I say unto you. That except your righteousness shall exceed the righteousness of the scribes and Pharisees, ye shall in no case enter into the kingdom of heaven* (Matthew 5:17-20).

Nothing has been done away with until the heavens and the earth melt with fervent heat in the end of age at the coming of the Lord.

The Lord stated that our righteousness must exceed that of the scribes and Pharisees. How do we become righteous or find out how to become righteous?

> *For they being ignorant of God's righteousness and going about to establish their own righteousness, have not submitted themselves unto the righteousness of God.*
>
> *for Christ is the goal of the law (torah) for the righteousness to every one that believeth.*

For Moses describeth the righteousness which is of the law (torah), that the man which doeth those things shall live by them (Romans 10:3-5).

So we need to go back to the torah to find out how God wants us to live. That is going back to the beginning to find out the end. Return to the old paths.

As Jeremiah puts it.

And it shall come to pass, if they will diligently learn the ways of my people, to swear by my name, The Lord liveth; as they taught my people to swear by Baal; then shall they be built in the midst of my people. But if they will not obey, I will utterly pluck up and destroy that nation, saith the Lord (Jeremiah 12:16-17).

This is saying that we are to learn the way of God's chosen people, Israel, to learn the ways of God. If we don't learn and obey Then He will pluck us up and destroy us. We will be cast into the pile of unwanted tares, ready for burning.

Ok, but what about the handwriting of ordinances it says that they were nailed to the cross?

Blotting out the handwriting of ordinances that was against us, which was contrary to us, and took it out of the way, nailing it to his cross (Colossians 2:14).

So, what are the handwriting of ordinances any way? When we continue to read the rest of the chapter we will find out just what they are. And they are not the commandments of God. So what are they? As we go on down to the 20 verse and start we will see.

Wherefore if ye were dead with Christ from the rudiments of the world, why, as though living in the world, are ye subject to ordinances (v. 20).

Touch not; taste not: handle not (v. 21).

Which all are to perish with the using; after the commandments and doctrines of men (v. 22).

These indeed have an appearance of wisdom in self imposed worship, humiliation and harsh treatment of the

> *body- of no value at all, only for the satisfaction of the flesh* (RSV)[31].

So, what are the handwriting of ordinances? They are any kind of laws by man to put us into bondage to one another that is not of God's Law.

The scribes and Pharisees of the day had their self-imposed rules to try and govern the people. But, the Master and Lord, shows that was not the way. So they set out to kill him, because He bucked their system. The Lord always walked in the teachings of His Father, but would not walk after the commandments of the leaders of His day.

Today we have the same things that go on in the so-called church world. The Leaders are always trying to impose their doctrines and agenda on the masses, sometimes by putting people on guilt trips when it is not the word of God, but a twisted form of the Word.

But why does God bless me?

Yes, God blesses and God curses. Anyone that practices the commandments and instructions that God set down in the beginning God will bless. But if we do not walk in the commandments and instruction that God has set down we will receive the curse. Let's turn to Deuteronomy 11.

> *Behold I set before you this day a blessing and a curse;*
>
> *A blessing, if ye obey the commandments of the Lord your God, which I command you this day:*
>
> *And a curse, if ye will not obey the commandments of the Lord your God, but turn aside out of the way which I command you this day, to go after other gods, which ye have not known* (Deuteronomy 11:26-27).

As we learn the commandments of the Lord God we choose to do them or not to do them.

Look at Deuteronomy 28 when we obey.

---

[31] Revised Standard Version of the Bible New Testament, Copyright 1952 by the Division of Christian Education, a Nation Council of the Churches of Christ in the United States of America.

And it shall come to pass, if thou shalt harken diligently unto the voice of the Lord thy God, to observe and to do all his commandments which I command thee this day, that the Lord thy God will set thee on high above all nations of the earth:

And all these blessings shall come on thee and overtake thee, if thou shalt hearken unto the voice of the Lord thy God (Deuteronomy 28:1-2).

Whenever we walk in all of the commandments of God He will pile the blessing on top of us that we won't be able to contain them all. But when we walk in our own ways, God will put the cursing on us. Not because God is putting them on us, but because we have chosen this thing and God only responds to our choosing of the blessing or the curse. Look at what God says in Deuteronomy 30.

And it shall come to pass, when all these things are come upon thee, the blessing and curse, which I have set before thee, and thou shalt call them to mind among all the nations, whether the Lord thy God hath driven thee.

And shalt return unto the Lord thy God, and thy shalt obey his voice according to all that I commanded thee this day, thou and thy children, with all thine heart, and with all thy soul.

That then the Lord thy God will turn thy captivity, and have compassion upon thee, and will return and gather thee from all the nations, whether the Lord thy God hath scattered thee (Deuteronomy 30:1-3).

So when we respond according to what God has set down, for us to live by then He, God will undo our captivity that we have gotten into.

God will bless anyone that practice any of the statutes that He has set down even if you don't know what they are. This is what is called by nature.

For when the Gentiles, (nations), which have not the law (torah), do by nature the things contained in the law

> *(torah), these, having not the law (torah), are a law unto themselves:*
>
> *Which show the work of the law (torah) written in their hearts, their conscience also bearing witness, and their thoughts the meanwhile accusing or else excusing one another* (Romans 2:14-15).

So what God does in this present age is He sends the rain on both the just and the unjust.

> *That ye may be the children of your Father, which is heaven: for he maketh his sun to rise on the evil and on the good, and sendeth rain on the just and the unjust* (Matthew 5:45).

So no matter if you are good or bad, and you practice the instructions of God, He will bless you in that area of your life. But you will at the same time receive cursing in other areas of your life until you turn and walk according to God's statutes and judgments, then He will undo and change your conditions in this area.

Look what Paul says in Romans.

> *But after thy hardness and impenitent heart treasurest up unto thyself wrath against the day of wrath and revelation of the righteous judgment of God:*
>
> *Who will render to every man according to his deeds:*
>
> *To them who by patient and continuance in well doing seek for glory and honor and immortality, eternal life:*
>
> *But unto them that are contentious, and do not obey the truth, but obey unrighteousness, indignation and wrath,*
>
> *Tribulation and anguish, upon every soul of man that doeth evil, of the Jew first and also the Gentile* (Romans 2:5-9).

So choose you this day, obedience to God to receive blessing or disobedience to receive cursing and the wrath of God to come, your choice.

CONCLUSION

The Lord God Almighty is Lord and Master of the Sabbath. It is time for His sheep to hear His voice and follow Him. That He may put them on the wings of Eagles and bring them unto Himself. Take hold of His holy day the Sabbath the seventh day of the week that you may ride upon the high places of the earth. When you hear His voice and walk in His ways He will cause you to ride on the wings of eagles and you will ride upon the high places of the earth and ride above the storm, while others will be riding in the storm.

The dragon, the devil, your adversary will become very angry with you when you begin to learn God's ways and walk in them up rightly, because you begin to keep the commandments of the living God, and the testimony of Jesus.

My people come out of Babylon and no longer be partakers of her deeds.

The way to come out of Babylon is to come to Jesus and learn of His ways and learn the ways of my people. Because straight and narrow is the way to life and few will find it, unless you return to the old paths that God, had set down in the beginning for you to follow you will not find your way. Contend for the Faith that was once delivered you. Jesus, the way, the truth, the life, the light, the living water, the bread of life, and the everlasting lamb that was slain from the foundation of the earth, Jesus your High Priest always interceding for His sheep. He is always waiting for His prodigal children to find their way home where you belong. Many of you have been lead astray by the Devil through his many devices and his luring you down the wrong paths.

Now is the time for repentance and turning to the Lord. Where do you stand now, if called home from this life to the next? Will it be on the Lord's side or the Devil's?

> *Ye shall have one law for him that sinneth through ignorance, both for him that is born among the children of Israel, and the stranger that sojourneth among them.*
>
> *But the soul that doeth aught presumptuously, whether he be born in the land, or a stranger, the same reproacheth the Lord; and that soul shall be cut off from among his people.*
>
> *Because he hath despised the word of the Lord, and hath broken his commandment, that soul shall utterly be cut off; his iniquity shall be upon him* (Numbers 15:29-31).

At what point or in what generation will there be a people that will begin to keep the covenant of the Father. How do we become that royal priesthood of people that God wants for Himself? This is how, look in Exodus

> *Now therefore, if ye will obey my voice indeed, and keep my covenant, then ye shall be a peculiar treasure unto me above all people: for all of the earth is mine:*
>
> *And ye shall be unto me a kingdom of priests, and a holy nation* (Exodus 19:5-6).

Before God will do many of the things that He swore to our forefathers at Mount Sinai, and to Abraham, we must learn to obey his voice and keep his covenant, than he will fulfill his oath. This is what He says in Jeremiah.

> *Hear ye the words of this covenant, and speak unto the men of Judah, and to the inhabitants of Jerusalem:*
>
> *And say thou unto them, thus saith the Lord God of Israel; cursed be the man that obeyeth not the words of this covenant,*
>
> *Which I commanded your fathers in the day that I brought them forth out of the land of Egypt, from the iron furnace, saying, Obey my voice, and do them, according to all*

which I commanded you: so shall ye be my people, and I will be your God.

That I may perform the oath which I have sworn unto your fathers, to give them a land flowing with milk and honey, and it is this day. Then I (Jeremiah) said, so be it, O Lord (Jeremiah11:2-5).

And so shall it be. When we begin to keep the covenant, then God will bring us once again unto Himself and bring us out of all of the nations of the earth that He scattered our fathers because of the transgressions that they committed against Him. And He will give His people the land that He told Abraham that his descendants would inherit.

This people will be the holy nation and the royal priesthood. And they will have made themselves ready as a bride makes herself ready to meet the bridegroom. And this people will be the remnant in the last days that will keep the commandment of God and the testimony of Jesus.

They will hear the voice of the Great Shepherd and will follow without question, because they have learned to keep the covenant of God.

When is the Rest?

After reading all this information, the only conclusion to come to, is, The Rest of God, the Sabbath, is when God said it would be to both the Jew and the Gentile. According to how God set it up. From sunset, Friday night, to sunset Saturday night, this is the way they do it in Jerusalem, The capital city of King David, the holy place of God. Which one-day, the New city of Jerusalem shall sit and all those that truly believe shall enter into the everlasting Rest.

The whole world wonders after the beast, who, is the beast, the Papal power in Rome, this is who the world seems to follow, It is this system that thinks to change Gods law and the world follows like blind sheep. Jesus says in Revelation 18:4 to come out of her my people that you may not be partakes of her sins, and that ye receive not of her plagues.

REVIEW QUESTIONS

With these questions it will help you better learn and understand God's will in this matter. With some of this question it will require us to go to the Bible and do some more digging to better understand. Be a student of the word.

1. Who are the forefathers of Israel?
2. When did the Gospel open up to the Gentiles (nations)?
3. When do you become Abraham's seed?
4. When did the word start?
5. What day did God sanctify?
6. What does it mean to sanctify something?
7. Whose ways are higher God's or ours?
8. What is it to hallow something and what was hallowed?
9. What are some of the meanings of law?
10. What does it mean to rest?
11. What should we not be doing on the Sabbath? Isaiah 58:13
12. Who did God say were a special people unto himself?
13. Where did God choose to put his name?
14. When we chose the Lord what are we to do?
15. When did the Gentiles get preached to? Acts 13:42
16. Who is God's chosen people?
17. What does it mean to have one law for you and the stranger?

18. What does it mean for a perpetual covenant?
19. What happens to the people that defile the Sabbath?
20. What are some of the things that God said the Sabbath would be?
21. Who is a stranger?
22. Whom do the Gentiles seek?
23. Who is among the Gentiles?
24. What did the people of the land become?
25. Who is a stranger today?
26. Who are aliens from the commonwealth of Israel?
27. What does God tell the stranger to do about His Sabbaths?
28. When we take hold of the Sabbath where do we ride?
29. What is it to pollute something?
30. What happens to the sheep?
31. How do you worship God in vain?
32. If we don't keep God's ordinance, what happens?
33. What is it that we profane? Ezekiel 22:8, 38
34. What are some of the things that the priest did in Ezekiel 22?
35. Why was Sodom and Gomorrah stoned?
36. Who is God going to take vengeance on?
37. What is to have a holy convocation?
38. What is more important to Mary than to Martha?
39. What is it that Israel would not find in the field?
40. What day was it that they would not find it?
41. What evil things where Judah doing on the Sabbath? Nehemiah 13
42. What kind of fire will there be for not hallowing the Sabbath?
43. What is the complaint of Amos 8?

44. Who's causing a famine and for what?
45. What were the people doing in the temple?
46. What kind of work did the priest do on the Sabbath?
47. Purifying yourself in Numbers 19 is a shadow of what in the New Testament?
48. What does the showbread represent?
49. Whom did Israel slay on the seventh day?
50. What kind of battle goes on, on the Sabbath?
51. List some of the things that Jesus did on the Sabbath?
52. Why did people rest on the Sabbath?
53. Who and what should have supreme dominion in our lives?
54. What did the people agree to?
55. God made known what to man?
56. When you have oxen what happens?
57. One thing that God is trying to tell us to do is what?
58. When people separated themselves unto the law of God what takes place?
59. About when was the book of Acts written?
60. What were they reading in the synagogue?
61. After the Jews left the synagogue, who came in and when did they come in.
62. Paul stayed in Thessalonica how long?
63. When did the city come together to hear the word of God?
64. In Acts 20:7 what time was in when the disciples came together to break bread?
65. Who transgressed the laws of God? Are you one of them?
66. What is happening in the new heaven and earth?
67. What is the sign between God and man and for how long?

68. How long is that?
69. What is the test for?
70. What are some of the promises that we receive by keeping God's commandments?
71. Where is the certain place that God spoke of the seventh day? Nehemiah 9
72. What does it mean to limit a certain day?
73. What are the old paths?
74. What happens when we take on Jesus yoke?
75. When we keep the Sabbath what are we rehearsing for?
76. How long is a day according to Peter?
77. What does God's Holy Days tell?
78. In the Maccabees what was being profaned?
79. What were the priest sacrificing?
80. Who is the dragon wroth with?
81. Does God change?
82. How long does God's commandments last?
83. What will happen if we change God's word?
84. In these last days what are we to remember?
85. What did Antiochus Epiphanes do?
86. What did Constantine do in 321A.D?
87. In 364A.D. the Catholic Church did what?
88. Sunday is the mark of whose authority?
89. What is being ignorant being likened to?
90. What did some of the church leaders have to say about change?
91. What is it to lay aside the commandments of God?
92. Who confound the languages?

93. How did Noah find grace in the eyes of God?
94. Colossians 4:12 say's we are to stand perfect in what?
95. What kind of testimony should I have?
96. How do we know God?
97. If we continue in sin what will happen?
98. What are the first five books of the Bible called?
99. Where is righteousness described at and who described it?
100. What does Jeremiah 12:16, 17 tell us we need to learn? And who is my people?
101. So what is the handwriting of ordinances that were done away with?
102. By what means does God bless a person?
103. Where are the commandments of God found?
104. By what means does God reward and punish on?

REFERENCES

1. The Winston Dictionary, copyright 1946, John C. Winston Co.
2. The American College Dictionary, copyright 1962, Random House N.Y.
3. Fossilized Customs, Strawberry Islands Publishers
4. The Oxford Annotated Bible with Apocrypha, copyright 1965, Oxford University Press
5. (1 Maccabees)
6. Strong's Exhaustive Concordance, Dugan Publishers Inc
7. Harper's Bible Dictionary, Harper & Row, Publishers, Inc. Copyright 1973
8. Peloubet's Bible Dictionary, Zondervan Publishing House, Copyright 1971
9. National Sunday Law by A. Jan Marcussen, 1990, published by Teach Services.

CHART OF THE WEEK

Chart of the week, which is included in the back, is extremely valuable and almost impossible to find. The following text is a quote from the chart of the week written by Vance Ferrell from Harvestime Books.

"Dr William Meade Jones lived over a hundred years ago, and was well known in London, England, research expert. He discovered in his studies that the seventh day Sabbath was the only weekly Sabbath ever commanded by God in the Bible.

> Jones decided since scripture clearly shows that the Bible Sabbath was first given to mankind at the end of creation week, If Genesis 2:1-3 is really true, then two important facts would have had to be known throughout the ancient world would:
>
> 1. a fixing of the seventh day weekly cycle on a worldwide basis,
> 2. an ancient world wide knowledge of the seventh day Sabbath,
>
> Jones was convinced of this for several reasons:
>
> > Adam and Noah were both earnest worshipers of God and would therefore have been faithful Sabbath keepers.
> >
> > They would have taught their descendents about the Bible Sabbath, who would be aware of its original sacredness.
> >
> > The truth that God is to be worship on the seventh of each seven day week requires a seven day weekly cycle. If the first generations kept the weekly Sabbath given at Creation, then their descendents would continue to keep a

seven-day week, even though they may have later turned to idols and left the true God.

Therefore, as the descendents of Adam and Noah spread out all over the world, they would have carried with them these two important facts:

Each week has seven days.

The seventh day of the week is the holy Sabbath given by God to mankind.

Another interesting truth would be that worshipers of the true God-the Creator God- would keep the seventh day Sabbath.

Even though many of Adams's and Noah's descendents would become scoffers, Jones reasoned, all of them would still carry with them twin truths of the six day creation week, of Genesis 1, by keeping of the seventh day weekly cycle, and the seventh day seventh day Sabbath rest, by naming the seventh day of the week in their language as their LANGUAGE as the SABBATH REST."

There is a PDF file on the internet.

Chart of the week showing the unchanged order of the days and the …" , this way you can view the whole chart in a larger format.

The **CHART OF THE WEEK**, which you now have in your hands, is over a hundred years old. ***It is extremely valuable and almost impossible to find today.*** We are reprinting it in this present form so that it can be given the widest possible distribution at the lowest cost. This will be the first time that, for greater clarity, it has been reprinted in two colors.

Dr. William Meade Jones lived over a hundred years ago, and was a well-known London, England, research expert. He discovered in his studies that the Seventh-day Sabbath was the only weekly Sabbath ever commanded by God in the Bible.

Jones decided that, since Scripture clearly shows that the Bible Sabbath was first given to mankind at end of Creation Week,—if Genesis 2:1-3 is really true, then two important facts would have had to be known throughout the ancient world would: First, a fixing of the seven-day weekly cycle on a world-wide basis, and second, an ancient world-wide knowledge of the Seventh-day Sabbath.

Jones was convinced of this for several reasons: 1—Adam and Noah were both earnest worshipers of God and would therefore have been faithful Sabbath keepers. 2—They would have taught their descendents about the Bible Sabbath, who would be aware of its original sacredness. 3—The truth that God is to be worshiped on the seventh of each seven-day week—requires a seven-day weekly cycle. If the first generations kept the weekly Sabbath given at Creation, then their descendents would continue to keep a seven-day week, even though they may have later turned to idols and left the worship of the True God. *4—Therefore, as the descendents of Adam and Noah spread out all over the world, they would have carried with them these two important facts: (1) Each week has seven days, and (2) the seventh day of the week is the holy Sabbath given by God to mankind.* (A third interesting truth would be that worshipers of the true God—the Creator God—would only be those that kept the Seventh-day Sabbath.) Even though many of Adam's and Noah's descendents would become scoffers, Jones reasoned, all of them would still carry with them the twin truths of the six-day Creation Week, of Genesis 1 (by their keeping of the seven-day weekly cycle, and the Seventh-day Sabbath rest (by naming the seventh day of the week in their language as the day of Sabbath rest).

Frank Meade Jones decided that if Genesis 1 and 2 were really true, and that if God really created the world in six days and then rested on the Seventh day,—then a majority of the languages of the world would prove the fact! And this, in turn, would be a powerful proof—not only that the Seventh day (and not the first day) was the true Sabbath of God—but also a dramatic proof that Genesis 1 and 2 are genuine—and that God is our Creator!

Thinking about both of these facts is stunning in the light of the abundance of corroborating evidence given on this amazing chart that proves them to be true!

Additional copies of this chart—to share as widely as possible—may be obtained on a donation basis from:

[redacted]

TRAIL GUIDES - ALTAMONT, TN 37301 USA

A Chart of the Week:

Shewing the UNCHANGED ORDER of the Days and the true Position of the SABBATH, as proved by the combined testimony of Ancient and Modern Languages.

CHART OF THE WEEK (BB-27)
PART ONE of a Two-part Chart Reprint
Published by
TRAIL GUIDES - Altamont, TN 37301

By WILLIAM MEAD JONES, D.D.

CHART OF THE WEEK
Page ONE of 4 pages
Published by
T. . IL GUIDES - Altamont, TN 37301

Abbreviations.—For "*r.l.*," read the foreign types from *right* to *left*; for "*t.b.*," read from *top* to *bottom*; read all others from *left* to *right*. The letter "*d.*" means that the language is *dead*. The various terms showing the place of the Sabbath, such as "purification-day," "bath-day," "Seventh-day," "end-day," &c., as well as "Sabbath," are indicated by figures in the extreme right-hand column. Literal translations are given and not equivalents, *e.g.*, "sa-sabt, the Sabbath," and not Saturday.

Pronunciation.—In reading the transliterations care should be taken to pronounce as nearly as possible after the following examples:—*â* (long) as in *father*; *ă* (short) as in *at*; *ā* (long) as *a* in *say*; *ĕ* (short) as in *ek* and *met*; *ī* (long) as in *machine* (never as *i* in *pine*); *ĭ* or *i* (short) as in *pin*; *ō* (long) as in *tone*; *ŏ* (short) as in *broke*; *ū* (long) as *oo* in *boon*, *room*, and *moon*; *ŭ* (short) is merely a shortened form of the same sound; *ai* as *eye*. Circumflex and acute accents lengthen vowels. All deviations from this system are adopted from authors.

ENTERED ACCORDING TO ACT OF CONGRESS, IN THE YEAR 1886, BY Rev. W. M. JONES, D.D., IN THE OFFICE OF THE LIBRARIAN OF CONGRESS, AT WASHINGTON, D.C., U.S.A.

No.	LANGUAGE, (Where Spoken, Read, or otherwise Used.)	WEEK, (Name of the Cluster, or Cycle, of Seven Days.)	1.	2.	3.	4.	5.	6.	Name of SEVENTH DAY (With Etymological Meaning.)	[illegible]
	Shemitic—									
1	Hebrew Bible. (World-wide)	(r.l.) שבוע shâ-vû-ah. Seven.	יום אחד yôm e-khâd. Day One.	יום שני yôm she-ni. Day Second.	יום שלישי yôm she-li-shî. Day Third.	יום רביעי yôm r'-vi-î. Day Fourth.	יום חמישי yôm kha-mi-shî. Day Fifth.	יום הששי yôm hash-shi-shî. Day the Sixth.	יום השביעי yôm hash-she-vî-î. Day the Seventh. / יום השבת yôm hash-shab-bath. Day the Sabbath.	1
2	Hebrew. (Ancient and Modern use.) (*Proceeding on to the Sabbath.)	(r.l.) שבועא shâ-vû-ah. Seven.	אחד בשבת e-khad be-shab-bath, One into* the Sabbath.	שני בשבת she-ni be-shab-bath. Second into the Sabbath.	שלישי בשבת she-li-shî be-shab-bath. Third into the Sabbath.	רביעי בשבת r'-vi-î be-shab-bath. Fourth into the Sabbath.	חמישי בשבת kha-mi-shî be-shab-bath. Fifth into the Sabbath.	ערב שבת קדש e-reb shab-bath ko-desh Eve of Holy Sabbath.	שבת shab-bath. Sabbath.	2
3	Targum of Onkelos. (Hebrew Literature.)	(r.l.) שבועא shâ-vû-ah. Seven.	יום חד yôm khad. Day One.	יום תנין yôm tin-yan. Day Second.	יום תליתאי yôm t'-li-thai. Day Third.	יום רביעאי yôm r'-vi-âi. Day Fourth.	יום חמישאי yôm kh'-mi-shai. Day Fifth.	יום שתיתאי yôm shi-thi-thai. Day Sixth.	יום שביעאה yôm sh'-vi-âh. Day Seventh. / שבת sab-bath. Sabbath.	3
4	Targum Dialect of the Jews in Kurdistan.	(r.l.) שבועא shâ-vû-ah. Seven.	יומת כשיבא yoy-met khay-shib-ba. Day One of the Seven.	יומת תורשב yoy-met t'-rû-shab. Day 2nd of the Seven.	יומת תלתשב yoy-met th'-lath-shab. Day 3rd of the Seven.	יומת ארבעשב yoy-met ar-bâ-shab. Day 4th of the Seven.	יומת חמשושב yoy-met kham-shû-shab, Day 5th of the Seven.	יומת ערובא yoy-met a-roy-ta. Day of Eve (of Sabbath).	יומת שבת קדיש yoy-met sha-bat ko-dash, Holy Sabbath Day.	4
5	Ancient Syriac. [illegible]	(r.l.) [illegible] shab-ba-tha. Sabbath.	[illegible] khad b'-shab-ba. One into* Sabbath.	[illegible] tren b'-shab-ba.* Two into Sabbath.	[illegible] th-la-tha b'-shab-ba. Three into Sabbath.	[illegible] ar-ba-th b'-shab-ba. Four into Sabbath.	[illegible] kham-sha b'-shab-ba. Five into Sabbath.	[illegible] 'a-rû-ba-tha, Eve (of Sabbath).	[illegible] shab-ba-tha. Sabbath.	5
6	Chaldee Syriac. vul. pronun. Kurdistan, and Oroomiah, Persia.	(r.l.) [illegible] yô-mat shap-tâ. Days into Sabbath.	[illegible] khad b'-shab-ba One into Sabbath.	[illegible] tren b'-shab-ba. Two into Sabbath.	[illegible] th-la-tha b'-shab-ba. Three into Sabbath.	[illegible] ar-ba b'-shab-ba. Four into Sabbath.	[illegible] kham-sha b'-shab-ba. Five into Sabbath.	[illegible] 'a-rû-ba-tha, and 'ro-ta. Eve (of Sabbath).	[illegible] shap-ta. Sabbath.	6
7	Samaritan. (Old Hebrew Letters.) Nablûs, Palestine.	(r.l.) [illegible] shâ-vû-âh. Seven.	[illegible] yô-ma khada Day One.	[illegible] yo-ma t'-ni-an Day Second.	[illegible] yo-ma t'-li-tha. Day Third.	[illegible] yo-ma r'-vi-âh, Day Fourth.	[illegible] yo-ma kha-mi-sha, Day Fifth.	[illegible] yo-ma shi-thi-tha. Day Sixth.	[illegible] yo-ma ha-sh'-vi-âh. Day the Seventh. / [illegible] shab-bath. Sabbath.	7

No.	Language	Week	Sunday	Monday	Tuesday	Wednesday	Thursday	Friday	Saturday
8	Babylonian, Euphrates and Tigris Valleys, Mesopotamia. (A written language 3800 B.C.) (d.)	Quarter of a Lunation.	First.	Second.	Third.	Fourth.	Fifth.	Sixth.	Seventh. Sabbath.
9	Assyrian, Euphrates and Tigris Valleys, Mesopotamia. (d.)	Quarter of a Lunation.	First.	Second.	Third.	Fourth.	Fifth.	Sixth.	Seventh. Sabbath.
10	Assyrian Planetary Names. (d.)	Ma-ai. Seven chiefs of the days of the week.	Double Star, or Regulus: the Sun.	The Star of A-nū-nit. The Moon.	The Star of Nergal. Mars.	The Star of Nebo. Mercury.	The Star of the King. Jupiter.	Brilliant Star of Mustelil. Venus.	The Star Zibanit. Saturn.
11	Arabia. (Very old names.)	(r.d.) Seven.	Business day.	Light Moon.	War Chief.	Turning day or Midweek.	Familiar or Society Day.	Eve (of Sabbath).	Chief or Rejoicing Day.
12	Arabic. (Ancient and Modern.) West. Asia, E., W. & N. Africa.	(r.d.) The Seven, Collection (of days).	The One (day).	The Two.	The Three.	The Four.	The Fifth.	Assembly (day, Moham.)	The Sabbath.
13	Maltese, Malta.	Ghimgh'a. Collection (of days).	H'add. One (day).	It-t'nien. Two (2nd day).	It-t'lieta. The 3 (3rd d.)	L'erbagh. The 4 (4th d.)	H'amis. Fifth (day.)	Il-gimgh'a. Assembly.	Is-sibt. The Sabbath.
14	Ge-ez or Ethiopic. Abyssinia. (Ge-ez signifies "original.")	Seven.	One (day).	Second.	Third.	Fourth.	Fifth.	Eve (of Sabbath).	Sabbath.
15	Tigre. Abyssinia. (Closely related to Ge-ez.)	Eight. The turn from the 7th or seven complete days. (comp. "une huitième" for week of 7 days.)	One (First day).	Second.	Third.	Fourth.	Fifth.	Eve (of Sabbath).	Sabbath.
16	Amharic, Abyssinia. (Nearly related to Ge-ez.)	Eight. (Same use as in Tigre).	One.	Second.	Third. "The other 2nd."	Fourth.	Fifth.	Eve (of Sabbath).	Sabbath.
17	Falasha. (Lang. of the Jews of Abyssinia.)		One.	Second.	Third.	Fourth.	Fifth.	Sixth.	The Sabbath.
	Hamitic—								
18	Old Egyptian. (Hieroglyphic). (d.)	No word found for Week. (Chons, Amen, At-hor and Seb also represent their respective Planets).	Ra. Sun.	Thoth. Chons. Moon.	Har chuta em chotchot. Mars.	Sebkau. Mercury.	Hor ap sheta. Amen. Jupiter.	Nuter tua. At-hor. Morning Star: Venus.	Hor Ka. Seb. Saturn.
19	Coptic. Egypt. (A dead language for 200 years.)	A period of time belonging to the Sabbath.	The First Day.	The 2nd Day.	The 3rd Day.	The Fourth Day.	The 5th Day.	The 6th Day.	The 7th Day. The Sabbath.
20	Orma or Galla. South of Abyssinia.	Seven.	Lady, Virgin Mary Day. Also Sanbata gudda (Rom. C.) Great or Festival Sabbath.	Second day. First Trade Day.	3rd Day to the Sabbath. Second Trade Day.	4th day to the Sabbath. Fourth (day).	Fifth (day).	Assembly (day).	Sabbath. Last day of the half-week inclusive of 4th day. Little, or Humble, or Solemn Sabbath. (A day of no ceremonial display and no work).
21	Tamashek or Towarek. Atlas Mountains, Africa.	(r.d.) Collection of Seven days.	First Day.	Second Day.	Third Day.	Fourth Day.	Fifth Day.	Assembly Day.	The Sabbath Day.
22	Kabyle or Berber. North Africa.	(r.d.) Seven (days).	Day the One (First).	Day the Two (2nd).	Day the Three (3rd).	Day the Four (4th).	Day the Fifth.	The Assembly day.	The Sabbath Day.
23	Hausa (Central Africa).	Seven Days.	The One (1st).	The Two (2nd).	The Three (3rd).	The Four (4th).	The Fifth.	The Assembly.	The Sabbath.
	Japhetic—								
24	Sanscrit. (The classic language of India.)	Seven.	Sun-day.	Moon-day.	Mars-day.	Mercury-day.	Jupiter-day.	Venus Star.	Saturn-day.
25	Hindi. India.	Seven.	Sun-day.	Moon-day.	Mars-day.	Mercury-day.	Jupiter-day.	Venus-day.	Saturn-day.
26	Pali. (The sacred language of India.)	Seven Days.	Sun-day.	Moon-day.	Mars-day.	Mercury-day.	Jupiter-day.	Venus-day.	Saturn-day.
27	Urdu or Hindustani. (Mohammedan and Hindu, India.)	(r.d.) Seven.	One to Sab. Sunday.	2nd to Sab. Moon-day.	3rd to Sab. Mars	4th to Sab. Mercury.	5th to Sab. Eve (of Juma).	Assembly (day).	Saturn Sabbath.
28	Sindhi. Sindh, India.	Seven.	Sun(day).	Moon(day).	Mars.	Mercury.	Jupiter.	Venus.	Saturn
29	Sindhi Mohammedan. Sindh, India.		Sun(day).	Moon(day).	Mars (day).	4th (day).	5th (day).	Assembly (day).	Saturn (day).
30	Gujarati. India.	Seven days.	Sun-day.	Moon-day.	Mars-day.	Mercury-day.	Jupiter-day.	Venus-day.	Saturn-day.

No.	LANGUAGE. (Where Spoken, Read, or otherwise Used.)	WEEK. (Name of the Cluster, or Cycle, or Seven Days.)	1.	2.	3.	4.	5.	6.	Name of SEVENTH DAY (With Etymological Meaning.)	Languages which directly refer to the Sabbath-day.
31	Marathi. India.	saptaha. Seven.	ravi-vâr. Sun-day.	som-vâr. Moon-day.	mangal-vâr. Mars-day.	bûdh-vâr. Mercury-day.	gûrû-vâr. Jupiter-day.	shûkra-vâr. Venus-day.	shani-vâr. Saturn-day.	
32	Cashmere. India.	(r.l.) hafta. Seven.	at-wâr. Sun-day.	sandar-wâr. Moon-day.	bong-wâr. Mars-day.	bôd-wâr. Mercury-day.	bris-wâr. Jupiter-day.	jûm-â. Assembly (day).	bat-wâr. Idolator's day.	
33	Punjabi. India.	sa-ta. Seven.	ayat-wâr. Sun-day.	som-wâr. Moon-day.	mângal-wâr. Mars-day.	bûdh-wâr. Mercury-day.	vîr-wâr. Jupiter-day.	sûkar-wâr. Venus-day.	bar. Day. (Bar is said of a door, a turn; perhaps of opening out and ending the another turn of seven days to begin.)	23
34	Punjabi Muhammadan. India.	hafta. Seven.	a-itwâr. Sun-day.	pîr. Moon. (old man).	mangal. Mars.	budh. Mercury.	jûmarat. Eve (of Jûmâ).	jûm-â. Assembly.	sanich-chhâr. Saturn.	
35	Bengali. India.	sâptaha. Seven.	rábi-vâr. Sun-day.	sôm-bâr. Moon-day.	mangal-bâr. Mars-day.	bûdha-bâr. Mercury-day.	brihaspati-bâr. Jupiter-day.	shûkra-bâr. Venus-day.	shani-bâr. Saturn-day.	
36	Assamese. Assam, India.	saptâha. Seven.	rabi-bâr. Sun-day.	som-bâr. Moon-day.	mangal. Mars.	budh-bâr. Mercury-day.	brihaspati-bâr. Jupiter-day.	sukur-bâr. Venus-day.	soni-bâr. Saturn-day.	
37	Uriya. Orissa, India.	sapoh and hapo. Seven.	rabi-bâr. Sun-day.	som-bâr. Moon-day.	mangal-bâr. Mars-day.	bûdh-bâr. Mercury-day.	gûrû-bâr. Jupiter-day.	shûkr-bâr. Venus-day.	sani-bâr. Saturn-day.	
38	Pashto or Afghan. Afghanistan.	(r.l.) al-isbûah. The seven.	yek-shamba. One to the Sabbath.	dû-shamba. Two to Sabbath.	sha-shamba. Three to Sabbath.	char-shamba. Four to Sabbath.	pânj-shamba. Five to Sabbath.	jûm-â. Assembly (day).	khâli. shamba. Unemployed-day, Holiday, Sabbath.	24
39	Pahlavi or Pûhlavi-Pazand. (Ancient Persian).	(r.l.) (1) shaba and (2) haft. Seven.	(1) mitra and (2) khûrshîd. Sun.	kamryâ. Moon.	(1) behram and (2) vahrân. Mars.	tîr. Mercury.	hormazd. Jupiter.	anâhita. Venus.	kêvan. Saturn. shambid, i.e., fragrance: The pleasantest day of the week. "Dies Sabbati." Sabbath.	25
40	Persian. Persia.	(r.l.) hafta. Seven (days).	yek-shambih. One to Sabbath.	dû-shambih. Two to Sabbath.	sih-shambih. Three to Sabbath.	chahâr-shambih. Four to Sabbath.	panj-shambih. Five to Sabbath.	âdîna. Religious (day).	shambih. Holiday, Sabbath.	26
41	Mythological. Persia and India.	Haft Rang. (Seven Colours.)	Yellow to the Sun.	Green to the Moon.	Red to Mars.	Blue to Mercury.	Brown to Jupiter.	White to Venus.	Black to Saturn.	
42	Armenian. Armenia.	shapat. Sabbath.	mia shapti. One to the Sabbath.	yergû-shapti. Second to the Sabbath.	yerek shapti. Third to the Sabbath.	chorek shapti. Fourth to the Sabbath.	hink shapti. Fifth of the Sabbath.	ûrpat. Fast Day.	shapat. Sabbath.	27
43	Kurdish. Kurdistan.	(r.l.) aĥftî. Seven.	yek-shamba. One to Sabbath.	dû-shamba. 2nd to Sabbath.	se-shamba. 3rd to Sabbath.	châr-shamba. 4th to Sabbath.	pani-shamba. 5th to Sabbath.	ainî. Religious day (Moham.)	shamba. Sabbath.	28
44	Brahuiky. Beluchistan.	(r.l.) hafta. Seven.	yek-shambé. One to Sab.	dû-shambé. 2nd to Sab.	sêi-shambé. 3rd to Sab.	chahâr-shambé. 4th to Sab.	panj-shambé. 5th to Sab.	jûm-â. Assembly.	awal-i-hafta. First or Chief of the Seven. shambé. Sabbath.	29
45	TARTARIC — Tungusian. Manchû. Manchûria. (Manchû and Chinese Characters.) Fac-simile of Manchû writing (full size) by a native of Manchûria. Sent from Peking in 1886. The Manchû alphabet is the same as the Mongolian with a few alterations.	The Mongolian Alphabet is the Manchû-Tartar Ouigour. The Turks used it before adopting the Arabian characters. It is derived from the Syriac Alphabet which was carried into Tartary by the Nestorian Missionaries in the 3rd century. "They filled Tartary and even China with their active propaganda." It is said that Syriac (Aramean) was originally written from top to bottom instead of horizontally as now. The Manchû and Mongol perpendicular lines proceed from left to right; the Chinese from right to left.	日 shûn. Sun (day).	月 bi-a. Moon (day).	火 ho-wo. wê-shi-ba. Mars-day.	水 mû-ke. wê-shi-ba. Mercury-day.	木 moo. wê-shi-ba. Jupiter-day.	金 ai-yeh. wê-shi-ba. Venus-day.	土 bol-buan. wê-shi-ba. Saturn-day.	
46	Mongolian. Sharra-Mongolian. Eastern Mongolia.	do-lo-ghan gô-nah, and dologan ho-nok: to pass the night; hence seven nights, an idiom for Seven days. comp. Old English use of se'night contracted from seven night (as fortnight from fourteen night) for seven nights and days.	a-dîl-ya. Sun.	sara. Princess, bright moon. Moon.	(1) (2) (1) li-li-gan. (2) gal-at-gâa. Planet Mars.	ba-lâ. Mercury.	(1) (2) (1) gigiratasain grak, and (2) var-has-ba-ti. Planet Jupiter.	(1) (2) (1) tsol-man. Morning Star. (2) sha-ga-sa. Venus.	na-ai-tsar, and bibsha. The Son of the Sun: Saturn. "The Mongols use 'Bimba' as another and especial term for the Seventh-day. They strictly keep it from the transaction of secular business. They neither give out nor take in any property at their homes, nor collect or pay debts, or start on a journey on that day."	30
47	Kalmuk. Western Mongolia.	do-lon gâ-rik. Seven Days.	na-ran gra-kê. Sun Planet.	soraiya. Moon.	mê-ga-mar gra-kê. Mars Planet.	ulburai gra-kê. Mercury Planet.	gi-lin-sêr gra-kê. Jupiter Planet.	basang gra-kê. Venus Planet.	bim-ba gra-kê. Saturn Planet. The centre or culmination of the other days.	31
48	Turkish. Osmanlian. Turkey.	sabô-ah. Seven.	bazar-gûni. Market Day.	bazar irtêsi. Morrow after Market.	sa-li. Third (Day).	châr shamba. Four to Sabbath.	panj. shamba. Five to Sabbath.	jûm-â. Assembly (day).	yôm-es-sabt. Day the Sabbath.	32

	Language	Week	Sunday	Monday	Tuesday	Wednesday	Thursday	Friday	Saturday	
49	Lama. Pashalik of Trebizond.					صاباتالدي Fourth to the Sabbath.		پاراسقه Preparation.	صابالون Sabbath.	33
50	Kezani-Tartar. Kazan, East Russia.	Day. (idiomatic for the same days.)	Market day.	2nd to the Sabbath.	3rd to the Sabbath.	4th to the Sabbath.	Fifth-day.	Assembly.	Hindmost of the series of Seven Days. Subbota. Sabbath.	34
51	Dravidian— Tamil. India.	[illegible] A Period of time.	[illegible] Sun-day.	[illegible] Moon-day.	[illegible] Mars-day.	[illegible] Bodh or Mercury-day.	[illegible] Jupiter-day.	[illegible] Morning Star or Venus-day.	[illegible] Saturn-day.	
52	Malayalam. India.	[illegible] Day circle (of Seven.)	[illegible] Sun-day.	[illegible] Moon-day.	[illegible] Mars-day.	[illegible] Mercury-day.	[illegible] Jupiter-day.	[illegible] Silence, Venus-day.	[illegible] Saturn-day.	
53	Kodaga or Coorg. Southern India.	[illegible] Seven days.	[illegible] Sun-day.	[illegible] Moon-day.	[illegible] Mars-day.	[illegible] Mercury-day.	[illegible] Jupiter-day.	[illegible] Venus-day.	[illegible] Saturn-day.	
54	Kanarese. India.	[illegible] Seven. A Day.	[illegible] Sun-day.	[illegible] Moon-day.	[illegible] Mars-day.	[illegible] Mercury-day.	[illegible] Jupiter-day.	[illegible] Venus-day.	[illegible] Saturn-day.	
55	Telugu. India.	[illegible] Space of Seven Days.	[illegible] Sun-day.	[illegible] Moon-day.	[illegible] Mars-day.	[illegible] Mercury-day.	[illegible] Jupiter-day.	[illegible] Venus-day.	[illegible] Saturn-day.	
56	Singhalese. Ceylon.	[illegible] Seven Days.	[illegible] Sun-day.	[illegible] Moon-day.	[illegible] Mars-day.	[illegible] Mercury-day.	[illegible] Jupiter-day.	[illegible] Venus-day.	[illegible] Saturn-day.	
57	Monosyllabic— Ancient Chinese. (Astronomical). Names of the Cycle of 28 days. It ever repeats itself without regard to years. This 7 and 28 day Cycle is used in China, Manchuria, Mongolia and Tibet.	七 ... 政 Or Seven Regulators, equivalent to Week. This method of reckoning the week is very old, and is a four-fold witness to the unchanged order of the series of seven days so well known in ancient and modern times. It has been a safeguard against the loss of a day of the week, and of one day being exchanged for another. Each day has its place assigned by four different planetary names.	1st Week 房 fang. Corresponding animal: Hare. 2nd Week 虛 hü. Corresponding animal: Rat. 3rd Week 昴 mao. Corresponding animal: Cock. 4th Week 星 sing. Corresponding animal: Horse. Sun.	1st Week 心 sin. Corresponding animal: Fox. 2nd Week 危 wei. Corresponding animal: Swallow. 3rd Week 畢 pih. Corresponding animal: Raven. 4th Week 張 chang. Corresponding animal: Deer. Moon.	1st Week 尾 wei. Corresponding animal: Tiger. 2nd Week 室 shih. Corresponding animal: Bear. 3rd Week 觜 tsui. Corresponding animal: Monkey. 4th Week 翼 yeh. Corresponding animal: Snake. Mars.	1st Week 箕 ki. Corresponding animal: Leopard. 2nd Week 壁 pih. Corresponding animal: Porcupine. 3rd Week 參 tsan. Corresponding animal: Ape. 4th Week 軫 chan. Corresponding animal: Worm. Mercury.	1st Week 斗 tau or dou. Corresponding animal: Griffin. 2nd Week 奎 kuei. Corresponding animal: Wolf. 3rd Week 井 tsing. Corresponding animal: Tapir. 4th Week 角 kioh. Corresponding animal: Dragon. Jupiter.	1st Week 牛 niu. Corresponding animal: Ox. 2nd Week 婁 leu. Corresponding animal: Dog. 3rd Week 鬼 kwei. Corresponding animal: Sheep. 4th Week 亢 k'ang. Corresponding animal: Dragon. Venus.	1st Week 女 nü. Corresponding animal: Bat. 2nd Week 胃 wei. Corresponding animal: Pheasant. 3rd Week 柳 liu. Corresponding animal: Muntjak. 4th Week 氐 ti. Corresponding animal: Badger. Saturn.	
58	Chinese (Roman Catholic). (Adopted long prior to those of the Protestant.)	li pai or lai pai.	瞻禮一 Day of looking up and worshipping.	瞻禮二 Worship-day Two.	瞻禮三 Worship-day Three.	瞻禮四 Worship-day Four.	瞻禮五 Worship-day Five.	瞻禮六 Worship-day Six.	瞻禮七 Worship-day Seven.	35
59	Chinese (Protestant). (Missionary names changed from the above, probably within a century.)	禮拜 li pai or lai pai.	禮拜日 Respectful, Worshipping.	禮拜一 Worship-day One.	禮拜二 Worship-day Two.	禮拜三 Worship-day Three.	禮拜四 Worship-day Four.	禮拜五 Worship-day Five.	禮拜六 Worship-day Six.	
60	Mohammadan Chinese. (Persian and Arabic Names.)	jŭm-ă. For want of space these native characters are placed horizontally.	[illegible] 1st to the Sabbath.	[illegible] 2nd to the Sabbath.	[illegible] 3rd to the Sabbath.	[illegible] 4th to the Sabbath.	[illegible] 5th to the Sabbath.	[illegible] Assembly.	[illegible] Sabbath.	36
61	Annamite. Annam.	[illegible] Kind or sort of ... Series of Days.	[illegible] Day in order the First.	[illegible] Day in order Two.	[illegible] Day in order Three.	[illegible] Day in order Four.	[illegible] Day in order Five.	[illegible] Day in order Six.	[illegible] Day in order Seven.	37
62	Tai—Siamese. Siam.	[illegible] Sun.	[illegible] Day Sun.	[illegible] Day Moon.	[illegible] Day Mars.	[illegible] Day Mercury.	[illegible] Day Jupiter.	[illegible] Day Venus.	[illegible] Day Saturn.	

CHART OF THE WEEK - Page TWO of 4 pages - Published by - TRAIL GUIDES - Altamont, TN 37301

We are thankful that this CHART OF THE WEEK can again be available—and now in three formats: [1] A 30x24 inch large, one-color, folded wall chart, [2] The same 30x24 inch wall chart, rolled and mailed in a tube, and [3] both sides of two 11x17 inch tracts. This third option is the most economical and is the only one available in two colors (black and deep red). The tracts are ideal for quantity distribution and are sent on a donation basis. If you are interested in the large wall charts, write for current costs of these materials. The CHART OF THE WEEK contains a message that should be shared as widely as possible, especially in this low-cost two-color tract format which includes additional historical and Biblical information about the Bible Sabbath and the weekly cycle. *But please feel free to reprint the Chart yourself, either on presses or photocopy machines!*

What are the facts about Sabbath and Sunday? For further information about the Bible Sabbath, write us for a copy of THIS IS THE BIBLE SABBATH [BS-6], WHO CHANGED THE BIBLE SABBATH [BS-2], THE STORY OF THE CHANGE OF THE SABBATH [BS-4-5], QUESTIONS AND ANSWERS ABOUT THE BIBLE SABBATH-PART 1-2 [BS-11-12], and HOW THE SABBATH WAS CHANGED TO SUNDAY [BS-26].

What are the facts about the weekly cycle? Has it continued unchanged since Creation? For much more information on this important topic, write us for a copy of DISCOVERING THE SABBATH OF JESUS [BS-3]

But if you want the fullest amount of information on all of this, send $2 for the 256-page book, BEYOND PITCAIRN. It is an unusually complete—and very readable—book on the entire Sabbath question. It will be sent to you postpaid.

For additional copies of this present two-part tract set, ask for CHART OF THE WEEK—PART 1-2 [BS-27-28]. All materials, except the book mentioned above, are sent on a donation basis.

This TWO-PART TRACT which you are now reading is CONCLUDED on the NEXT tract in this series, which is CHART OF THE WEEK—PART 2 [BS-28].

TRAIL GUIDES - ALTAMONT, TN 37301 USA

77	Suanian. Caucasus.	There were 150 languages spoken in the Caucasus in Pliny's time.	Day One.						Sabbath.	43
78	Ingoush. Caucasus.		Lordly (day.)			Four.		Preparation.	Sabbath.	44
79	Aware or Avar (Daghestan.) Cis-Caucasus.	Seven.		Second day.			Fifth-day.		Sabbath Day.	45
80	Circassian. Circassia.	(r.l.) Space of Seven Days.	Market-day.	Morrow after Market.	Djerid.	Space of Four days.	Space of Five days.	Day of Assembly.	Morrow after Assembly.	
81	POLYNESIAN.— Malayan. Sumatra.	(r.l.) Collection (of Days.)	Day One.	Day Two.	Day Three.	Day Four.	Day Fifth.	Day Assembly.	Day Sabbath.	46
82	Javanese. Java.	Collection of Days.	Day One.	Day Two.	Day Three.	Day Fourth.	Day Fifth.	Day (of the) Assembly.	Sabbath.	47
83	Sunda (West Java.)	Collection (of Days).	One (day).	Two (2nd day).	Three (3rd day).	Fourth (day).	Fifth.	Assembly (d.)	Sabbath.	48
84	Dayak. Borneo.		Day One.	Day Two.	Day Three.	Day Fourth.	Day Fifth.	Day of Assembly.	Sabbath.	49
85	Makasar. Southern Celebes and Salayer Islands.	Seven.	One.	(Day) Two.	(Day) Three.	(Day) Fourth.	(Day) Fifth.	Assembly (Day).	Sabbath.	50
86	Bugis. Celebes.	Seven.	One	Two.	Three.	Four.	Fifth.	Assembly.	Sabbath.	51
87	Malagasy. Madagascar.	Complete Measure.	The One (day).	The Second (day).	Three (3rd day).	The Fourth (day).	The Fifth (day).	Assemuly.	The Sabbath.	52
88	Nuforian. N.W. New Guinea.	Day in Seven. (Time of Seven Days.)	Day (One)	Day Two.	Day Three.	Day Four.	Day Five.		Day Seven.	53
89	AFRICAN.— Swahili. East Equatorial Africa.	Collection of (Days).	The One (Day).	The Two (Day).	The Three.	The Fourth (Day).	The Fifth (Day).	Assembly (Day).	The Sabbath.	54
90	Congo. West Equatorial Africa.	The Negroes of the Gold Coast say, "God, the Creator, made Seven Days."	Domingo.	2nd Market Day.	3rd Feira (fair) or 3rd Market Day.	4th Feria, or 4th Market Day.	5th Feira, or 5th Market Day.	6th Feira, or 6th Market-day.	Saturday. Sabbado: Sabbath.	55
91	ISOLATED LANGUAGES— Wolof. Senegambia, West Africa.	Seven.	Dimanche.	The Two.	Three.	The Four.	The Fifth.	The Assembly (Day).	Last Day. Sabbath.	56
92	Fulah (West Africa.)				Three (3rd day).	The Four (4th d.)		The Assembly.	The Sabbath.	57
93	Mandingo. South of Senegal, West Africa.		The One.	Two.	Three.	The Four.	The Fifth.	The Assembly.	Sabbath.	58
94	Teda. Central Africa.	Collection of Days.	The One.	The Two.	Three.	The Fourth.	The Fifth.	The Assembly.	The Sabbath.	59
95	Bornu or Kanuri. Central Africa.	Collection.	The One.	The Two.	Three.	The Fourth.	The Fifth.	Assembly.	Sabbath.	60
96	Fulfulde. Central Africa.		The One.	The Two.	The Three.	The Fourth.	The Fifth.	The Assembly.	The Sabbath.	61
97	Sonrai. Central Africa.		The One.	The Two.	The Three.	The Fourth.	The Fifth.	The Assembly.	The Sabbath.	62
98	Logone. Central Africa.	Seven Days.	The One.	The Two.	The Three.	The Fourth.	The Fifth.	The Assembly.	The Sabbath.	63
99	Wandala. Central Africa.		The One.	The Two.	Three.	The Fourth.	The Fifth.	Assembly	Sabbath.	64
100	Bagirmi. Central Africa.	Collection.	The One.	The Two.	Three.	The Fourth.	The Fifth.	The Assembly.	Sabbath.	65
101	Maba. Central Africa.	Seven.	One.	The Two.	The Three.	Fourth.	Fifth.	Assembly.	Sabbath.	66
102	MISCELLANEOUS— Norman French. (10th and 11th Centuries.)	Sepmayn, Sepmaine.	Diemaine.	Lener.	Jeusday, Jeusdye, Juriadie.	Merkedy, Mercuredi, Mercdie, Meskerdy	Jeadi.	Venerdy, Venardy, and Vanredi.	Sabbedi, Samaday, Semadi, Sabbath Day.	67
103	Ancient French. (12th and 13th Centuries.)	Semaine, Semeigne.		Lundi.	Marsdi.	Merquedi.	Joedi, Jeusdi.	Vendredi, Vendresdi.	Samedi i.e. Sabbath Day.	68
104	D'oc. France. (Ancient and Modern).	Seven Days.	Day Dominical.	Day Moon (White-day.)	Day Mars.	Day Mercury.	Day Jupiter.	Day Venus.	Day Sabbath.	69
105	Ecclesiastical. Roman.		Dominica.	Feria Secunda.	Feria Tertia.	Feria Quarta	Feria Quinta.	Feria Sexta.	Sabbatum.	70
106	Parliamentary. British.	Until recently whenever Parliament assembled on Saturday, the Clerk wrote the day of the week thus—"Dies Sabbati."	Dies Solis.	Dies Lunae.	Dies Martis.	Dies Mercurii.	Dies Jovis.	Dies Veneris.	Dies Sabbati.	71
107	Astronomical.		☉ Sun.	☾ Moon.	♂ Mars.	☿ Mercury.	♃ Jupiter.	♀ Venus.	♄ Saturn.	

THE DAYS OF THE WEEK IN ALL THE EUROPEAN LANGUAGES.

242	Dutch (Holland).	Week	Zondag	Maandag	Dingsdag	Woensdag	Donderdag	Vrijdag	Zaturdag (Saturday).	
143	[illegible] Holland.	Wike	[illegible]	[illegible]	[illegible]	Wansdei	Thongersdei	Freedei	Snênd Corruption of High German Sonnabend, q.v.	
144	English (England).	Week	Sunday	Monday	Tuesday	Wednesday	Thursday	Friday	Saturday (Saturn-day).	
145	Icelandic (Iceland).	Vika	Sunnudagur	Mánudagur	Þriðjudagur	Miðvikudagur	Fimmtudagur	Föstudagur	Laugardagur (of bath-day).	94
146	Swedish, Sweden.	Vecka	Söndag	Måndag	Tisdag	Onsdag	Thorsdag	Fredag	Lördag Corruption of Icelandic Laugardagur, q.v.	95
147	Danish. Denmark.	Uge	Søndag	Mandag	Tirsdag	Onsdag	Torsdag	Fredag	Løverdag Corruption of Icelandic Laugardagur, q.v.	96
148	Old Slave (Bulgaria). (d)	Sedmica, Sedmina	Nedělja, Voskresénie	Ponedjéljnik	Vtórnik	Sredá	Četvrg, Četvertók	Pjatók	Subbota (Sabbath)	97
149	Russian (Russia).	Nedjelja	Voskresenje	Ponedjeljnik	Vtornik	Sereda	Četvertok	Pjatnica	Subbota (Sabbath).	98
150	Illyrian (Dalmatia, Servia).	Nedjelja	Nedjelja	Ponedeljak	Utorak, Vtornik	Srieda	Četvrtak	Petak	Subota (Sabbath).	99
151	New Slovenian, Illyria, in Austria.	Tèden, Tjèden, Kèden	Nedèlja	Ponedèljek	Tork, Vtork	Sréda	Četertek	Pétek	Sobóta Sabbath.	100
152	Bulgarian (Bulgaria).	Nedjelja	Nedjelja	Ponedjelnik	Vtornik	Srjeda	Četvrtak	Petak	Sàbbota (Sabbath).	101
153	Polish (Poland).	Tydzień, Niedziele, pl.	Niedziela	Poniedziałek	Wtorek	Środa	Czwartek	Piątek	Sobota (Sabbath).	102
154	Bohemian (Bohemia).	Týden, Neděle, pl.	Neděle	Pondělek	Úterek	Středa	Čtvrtek	Pátek	Sobota (Sabbath).	103
155	Lusatian (Saxony).	Tydźeń, Njedźele, pl.	Njedźela	Póndźela	Wutora	Srjeda	Štwórtk	Pjatk	Sobota (Sabbath).	104
156	Polabic. (A.) Borders of the Elbe.	Nedèla	Nedèla	Paddéla, Pacéla, Pocél.	Tórj	Sóda	Pérèndie	Škópj	Sóbóta Sabbath.	105
157	Lithuanian (Prussian Lithuania).	Nedėlia, Neddèlia	Nedėlia	Panedėlis	Utarninkas	Sereda	Ketverges	Pėtnyczia	Subata (Sabbath).	106
158	Prussian (Prussia). (d).		Naddele	Ponadèle		Possissawaite	Ketwirtice	Pentinx	Sabatico (Sabbath).	107
159	Lettish (Baltic Russia).	Neddela	Svèdina	Pirmdina	Otrdina	Trešdiena	Zettortdina	Piekdina	Sesdina (Sixth-day of week).	
160	English Bible	Week.	The First Day.	The Second Day	The Third Day.	The Fourth Day	The Fifth Day.	The Sixth Day	The Seventh Day, The Sabbath.	108

CHART OF THE WEEK - Page FOUR of 4 pages - Published by - TRAIL GUIDES - Altamont, TN 37301

1—SOME FACTS ABOUT THE BIBLE SABBATH —

At the close of Creation Week (Gen 1) God rested on the Seventh-day and hallowed and blessed it (Gen 2:1-3). This is God's own day—His special day—the Lord's day. Jesus Christ created all things (Col 1:16; Jn 1:3; Heb 1:1-3) and He calls Himself the Lord of the Sabbath (Mk 2:28). It is His day, the Lord's Day. He made it for man—all mankind (Mk 2:27) and not just the Jewish race.

The Sabbath was given to man at the Creation of the world (Gen 2:1-3), and His followers kept it (Ex 16) **before it was proclaimed** on Mount Sinai (Ex 20:8-11). It is the **seal** of the law and the sign that He is our Creator (Ex 31:17), our Redeemer (Ex 20:12), and that we belong to Him (Ex 20:20).

While here on earth, Jesus gave us a careful example of obedience to the Sabbath law He had given mankind (Lk 4:16), and rebuked man-made changes in His laws (Matt 15:9,6). He magnified the law and made it honorable (Isa 42:21).

Just before His death He predicted the destruction of Jerusalem 39 years later, in A.D. 70, and the end of the world (Matt 24), and He told His followers to continue to keep the Sabbath when those terrible events would happen years and even centuries later (Matt 24:20).

He carefully instructed His disciples to keep His day holy, for He wanted them to keep it after His sacrifice on Calvary. His followers faithfully kept it after His death (Lk 23:56), and later in their missionary work (Ac 13:14-16, 40-46; 16:12-15; 17:1-4). They declared that we ought to obey God rather than men (Ac 5:29), and Paul could sincerely say, "Do we make void the law through faith? God forbid: yea, we establish the law." (Rom 3:31). The promise of God was being fulfilled that Gentiles would keep the Sabbath the Jews were desecrating. (Isa 56:3-7).

The Bible predicted that a church-state power would arise in later centuries that would seek to destroy the atonement and God's laws from among His people (Dan 7:3, 20-21, 25; 8:9-12). The attempt by this power to change God's laws, and especially His time law—the Sabbath—was specifically predicted in Daniel 7:25. Only God can change the law, and so Paul predicted the rise of a man who would call himself god; (2 Thess 2:3-4). This organization would pretend to sit in God's temple calling itself god (2 Thess 2:4), and boastfully admitting its change in God's law from the seventh day to the first—and declare that this act was the Mark of its authority! And, indeed, is it not?

"Whom ye obey, his servants ye are." (Rom 6:16). God's Word declares that obedience to this man-made god by keeping his counterfeit—substitute—day of worship, while knowing that there is not one word or one hint in all *Scripture* to support such worship—will soon bring upon oneself the Mark of the Beast (Rev 13:16-17, 14:6-12). Only the remnant people of God in the last days, who keep the commandments of God and the faith of Jesus will at that time resist it (Rev 13:8; 14:6-12; 12:17). In fact, the Bible predicts a return to the true Sabbath as God's people will rebuild the torn-out place in the law of God—by again keeping His true Sabbath (Isa 58:13-14). And, thank God, the assuring prophecy is given that the assuring prophecy is given us that the saved of all ages will one day soon, honor the holy Sabbath of God for all eternity in the new earth (Isa 66:22-23).

Sunday is never called sacred or holy anywhere in the Bible. It is never called the *Sabbath* or the Lord's Day. Sunday is mentioned only eight times in the Bible, and none of them is a command by the God of heaven transferring the sabbath sacredness to the first day of the week. (Gen 1:5; Matt 28:1; Mk 16:1-2,9; Lk 24:1; Jn 20:1,19).

The Seventh-day Sabbath is the Day of the Lord—the Lord's Day (Rev 1:10; Ex 16:23,25; 31:15; 35:2; Ex 20:10; Lev 23:3; Deut 5:4). It is His own day (Isa 58:13) which He wants to share with you. *He plans* to keep it with you through all eternity to come (Isa 66:22-23). Come, worship Him on the best day—His day—the only day of weekly worship your God ever gave to you.

2—SOME FACTS ABOUT THE WEEKLY CYCLE —

Is the seventh day of the week today is the same as in the time of Christ and Moses? This is very important. The seven-day week, as well as the Bible Sabbath that terminates it, had a common origin in history. Both originated at the Creation of our world. Scientists, historians, and astronomers affirm that the seven-day weekly cycle has continued uninterrupted on down to our own day.

BIBLE—God has had faithful worshipers who have kept the Sabbath on down from the beginning of the world. But if time had been lost, the Divine Lawgiver would have set the matter aright when the Ten Commandments were given on Mount Sinai (1450 B.C.). (Ex 20). The experience in Exodus 16, which occurred before Sinai, illustrates the importance of keeping the Bible Sabbath. If the Sabbath had been lost between Moses' time and that of Christ, we would have the example of Christ (Lk 4:16,31; Jn 15:10). If time or the Sabbath had been lost, Jesus would have found it for His followers. The events of the crucifixion help fix the Sabbath (Lk 23:54-56; Mk 15:42; Lk 23:54,56).

THE CALENDAR—The Julian calendar was in use when Jesus was on earth. This calendar, which continued in use for 15 centuries was not accurate in the length of its year, for it was a quarter-hour too long. By 1582, it was 10 days off. The Gregorian calendar was started in that year for some of the nations of Europe. Others did not change over for 200 years thereafter, but all that time the weekly cycle continued unchanged. The length of the year was changed, but the week was not.

SCIENTISTS, HISTORIANS, AND ASTRONOMERS—We do not have space to discuss the evidence here, but researchers in these fields support the continuity of the seven-day weekly cycle since earliest times. *See "No Time Lost" in our book, BEYOND PITCAIRN, for much more information on this.*

THE JEWISH RACE—Our heavenly Father has given us more than scientific and historical evidence, He has given us the Jewish race! Every other Near East ethnic group has disappeared—the Hitites, Sumarians, Babylonians, Assyrians, Moabites, Philistines,—but the Jews remain, and with them the Seventh-day Sabbath. They have faithful kept it since the time of Moses, 3400 years ago. Any Jew will tell you that the seventh day is the Sabbath—and that it falls on Saturday of each week.

The commands of God are simple and require our obedience.

TRAIL GUIDES - ALTAMONT, TN 37301 USA

CHART OF THE WEEK [BS-27]
PART TWO of a Two-part Chart Reprint
Published by
TRAIL GUIDES - Altamont, TN 37301

A Chart of the Week:

Showing the UNCHANGED ORDER of the Days and the true Position of the SABBATH, as proved by the combined testimony of Ancient and Modern Languages.

By WILLIAM MEAD JONES, D.D.

CHART OF THE WEEK
Page THREE of 4 pages
Published by
TRAIL GUIDES - Altamont, TN 37301

No.	LANGUAGE. (Where Spoken, Read, or otherwise Used.)	WEEK. (Name of the Cluster, or Cycle, of Seven Days.)	1.	2.	3.	4.	5.	6.	Name of SEVENTH DAY (With Etymological Meaning.)
63	Kambojan. (Khmer.) Kamboja.	Sun. [By extension, seven days.]	Day Sun.	Day Moon.	Day Mars.	Day Mercury.	Day Jupiter.	Day Venus.	Day Saturn.
64	Mranma or Burmese. Birmah.	Seven Days.	Day devoted to the Sun. (One day thou to the Sun.)	One thou to the Moon.	Mars.	Mercury.	Jupiter.	Venus.	Saturn.
65	Ancient Peguan. Pegu-Burmah.	Seven (days).	(Day) One.	(Day) Two.	(Day) Three.	(Day) Four.	(Day) Five.	(Day) Six.	(Day) Seven.
66	Modern Peguan. Burmah.	Seven (days).	Sun (day).	Moon (day).	Mars (day).	Mercury-day.	Jupiter-day.	Venus (day).	Saturn (day).
67	Shan. Burmah.	Seven Days.	Sun-day.	Moon-day.	Mars (Day).	Mercury-day.	Jupiter-day.	Venus-day.	Saturn (Day).
68	Manipuri. South of Assam.	Seven.	Sun.	Moon.	Mars.	Mercury.	Jupiter.	Venus.	Saturn.
69	Khassi. Cossyah Hills, East of Bengal.	Ka shi taiew. A Seven days.	Ka sngi U Blei. A day devoted to the Sun.	Ka sngi sombar. Moon-day.	Ka sngi bat Majai. A day to Mars.	Ka sngi balang. Mid-week.	Ka sngi kaba san. A day the Fifth.	Ka sngi thoh-ding.	Ka sngi sait-jain. Purification-day.
70	Ancient Rong or Lepcha. Darjeeling and Sikkim Hills, East of Nepal and South of Tibet.	A Period of Seven Days.	Fire Day.	Water Day.	War Planet Day.	Copper Planet Day.	Wood Planet Day.	Gold Planet Day.	Earth Planet Day.
71	Modern Rong or Lepcha.	A Period of Seven Days.	Planet Sun.	Planet Moon.	Planet Mars.	Planet Mercury.	Planet Jupiter.	Planet Venus.	Planet Saturn.
	Isolated Languages:—								
72	Japanese. Japan.	A turn, a period of 7 days.	Sun-day.	Moon-day.	Mars-day.	Mercury-day. (Water).	Jupiter-day. (Wood).	Venus-day. (Gold).	Saturn-day. (Copper)
73	Corean.	The names of the Corean ... correspond with the four weeks cycle of the Chinese.	Sun.	Moon.	Fire Star. Mars.	Water Star. Mercury.	Wood Star. Jupiter.	Metal Star. Venus.	Earth Star. Saturn.
74	Tibetan. Tibet.	One Seven Days.	Planet Sun.	Planet Moon.	Planet Mars.	Planet Mercury.	Planet Jupiter.	Planet Venus.	(Planet Seven). The Seventh Planet. Saturn.
75	Bhotan. Little Tibet.	Planet days Seven. Days Seven.	Planet Day. Planet Sun.	(Darkness bracket). Planet Moon.	(Eye red). Mars.	Half-week Planet. Planet Mercury.	Jupiter.	Planet Venus.	Eye of God—Saturn. Seventh Brilliant Star.
76	Georgian. Caucasus.	Seven. Also shabati: Sabbath.	Lordly (day.)	Two to the Sabbath.	Three to the Sabbath.	Four to the Sabbath.	Five to the Sabbath.	Preparation (day).	Sabbath.

God's Law vs Papal Law

Sabbath Law vs Sunday Law

> *Jesus came and spoke unto them, saying, all power is given me in heaven and earth.* (Matthew 28:18).

vs

The Pope says God gave him the authority to make the changes in God's law

Who should we follow Jesus or the Pope?

> *Therefore, the son of man is Lord even of the Sabbath* (Mark 2:28).
>
> *Then He told them, the son of man is Lord of the Sabbath* (Luke 6:5).

John said in Revelation 1:10, *"I was in the Spirit on the Lord's Day."*

So what day would John be in the Spirit on? Would it not be the Sabbath Day (Saturday) and not Sunday?

The pope claims Sunday as the day of the Lord and not the Sabbath.

ONCE AND FOR ALL, A CONSTANT CALENDAR

BY JOHN M. CULKIN (an executive director of the Center for Understanding Media, in New York City.)
(emphasis and note added by Gary C. Michael)

You can't count on our current calendar. Every year, the numbered dates fall on a different day of the week. The average American has to check a calendar, a watch or ask a stranger to determine what day a particular date falls on - whether, for instance Jan. 31st a Saturday or a Wednesday. You have to use fingers, toes and other calculators to determine how many days are in a particular month. Even serious adults are occasionally caught reciting a bad rhyme to figure out the cycles.

The problem is that the months are uneven, 28 days in one month, 30 or 31 in others. As a result ***we have 14 different calendar arrangements. In short, the current calendar doesn't do well what a calendar should do - reckon time clearly and consistently so we can easily mark the past, locate the present and predict the future.***

It's time to make a year as neat and predictable as the day, to tidy up the internal year (days, weeks, months) as Julius Caesar and Gregory XIII synchronized the external calendar year with the solar year. It's time for a single, permanent calendar that gives us one formula, which can be learned once and used forever - ***the constant calendar.***

Over the last 60 years, the League of Nations and the United Nations considered the adoption of a couple of calendars that attempted (unsuccessfully, in my opinion) to solve the problems caused by our present calendar. Many business and accounting firms use some variation of a 52-53 week calendar to even out the year for financial reporting purposes. ***The Constant Calendar is designed to be user - friendly*** and to make life easier for you and me as well as for the certified public accountants.

This simplified calendar would divide the year into four quarters, each having 28-day months and one 35-day month. Dates would always fall on the same day of the week. ***For instance, the first day of the month would ALWAYS be Monday and the 28th day would ALWAYS be a Sunday. All weeks would begin on Monday and the days of the weekend would be at week's end.***

It adds up to 364 days. The 365th day, dec. 36, would fall between Sunday and Monday and would be called an INTERCALATED day, a blank day or a "tween day" (in between). It could be a holiday - World Peace Day, perhaps. In leap years, the extra day would be added in a similar fashion as a holiday at the end of June.

Thus we get clean and equal quarters (3 months, 13 weeks, 91 days), a fixed match of days and dates, ***an easy to remember*** structure and a relatively simple process of adjustment.

The major holidays also cooperate nicely by falling into convenient patterns - New Year's Day (Jan. 1) would ***always*** be a Monday of a four-day weekend (Including Dec. 36, the annual holiday); Memorial Day (May 22) would be the last Monday of the month; Independence Day (July 4), a Thursday; Labor Day (Sept. 1), Thursday; and Christmas (Dec. 25), ***always*** a Thursday. Moreover, we eliminate forever, for those who are concerned, the prospect of Friday the 13th.

Some people would be more inconvenienced than others. ***Calendar-makers would soon realize that the public would still want a monthly change of scenery and that there would be profits made in producing a constant calendar as an art form.*** Astrologers would manifest their wonted flexibility in adjusting their charts to the new calendar. Movable feasts based on the moon would find their place within the new structure, as they have in the past. And the 5 percent of the population whose birthdays fell on the 29th, 30th, and 31st days of the old calendar could opt under the new 28 day months for celebrating on the 28th of the month or an early day of the next month - or both.

As culture changes go, the shift to this new calendar would be a serious but not a traumatic event. The ***United Nations*** should be able to debate it and vote decisively on it within a dozen years or so.

The perfect time to introduce the Constant Calendar would be Jan. 1, 2001 - the first day of a new year, a new century and a new millennium. That would allow time for discussion and adjustment. It is also a year in

POPE JOHN PAUL'S PROPOSED JUBILEE 2000 CALENDAR TO START IN 2001 (ONCE AND FOR ALL, A CONSTANT CALENDAR)

OUR CURRENT CALENDAR (GREGORIAN CALENDAR)

SUN	MON	TUE	WED	THU	FRI	SAT
1	2	3	4	5	6	7

TRANSITION FROM CURRENT CALENDAR TO NEW CONSTANT CALENDAR

SUN	MON	TUE	WED	THU	FRI	SAT	Transition extra day SUN	MON	TUE	WED	THU	FRI	SAT	SUN
1	2	3	4	5	6	7	1	1	2	3	4	5	6	7

1st QUARTER OF CONSTANT CALENDAR

JANUARY

MON	TUE	WED	THU	FRI	SAT	SUN
1	2	3	4	5	6	7
8	9	10	11	12	13	14
15	16	17	18	19	20	21
22	23	24	25	26	27	28

FEBRUARY

MON	TUE	WED	THU	FRI	SAT	SUN
1	2	3	4	5	6	7
8	9	10	11	12	13	14
15	16	17	18	19	20	21
22	23	24	25	26	27	28

MARCH

MON	TUE	WED	THU	FRI	SAT	SUN
1	2	3	4	5	6	7
8	9	10	11	12	13	14
15	16	17	18	19	20	21
22	23	24	25	26	27	28
29	30	31	32	33	34	35

NOTE: This calendar would not be a problem with God if they were not planning on changing the weekly cycle. But they are planning just that. By making Monday instead of Sunday the first day of the week, they shift the beginning of the cycle one day to the right on the calendar. Since the sequence of the days remains unchanged, **Saturday** is still the true 7th day. They will simply call it the 6th day. Pray that God's people will not be deceived. We've been **WARNED** for a long time now to look out for this. This is soon to come upon us like a bad storm. **GET READY! GET READY! GET READY!**

NEWS ARTICLES

GC 588. Like with the capture and trial of dear Jesus, once the devil brings his Sunday movement into the open - he will keep pushing it, and this issue won't go under cover like it has been. In the past I've wondered who Satan will use to bring the issue into the open and start pushing it. Would he get his chief apostle to do it? You can imagine how long it would take for "Protestants" and Rome to join in that push. How long will it take before it comes right out in newspapers around the world that he is openly saying to keep Sundays holy?

Newsday, Wed. July, 8, 1998.

Pope: Keep Sundays holy

VATICAN CITY: Pope John Paul, in a letter to the world's one billion Catholics, urged them yesterday to rediscover Sundays as not just part of the weekend but a day dedicated to God, the family and healthy entertainment.

"What the letter says is that there should be no impediments to Christians to take part in Sunday worship and make holy the day of the lord," the bishop said.

In many parts of the world, particularly in developed nations, "the percentage of those attending the Sunday liturgy is strikingly low", the Pontiff lamented.

The Pope struck a paternalistic rather than authoritarian tone in the letter, saying he realised the pressures of modern society often made it difficult to keep Sundays religious.

San Jose Mercury News, Wednesday, July 8, 1998

Pope lays down law

■ Sabbath: Skipping Sunday services is a "grave sin"

Washington Post

VATICAN CITY — The Pope said that the "holiness of the Lord's day" must be protected at all costs.

"If after six days of work - people look for time to relax and pay more attention to other aspects of their lives, this corresponds to an authentic need which is in full harmony with the vision of the Gospel message," the Pope wrote. "In any case, they are obliged in conscience to arrange their Sunday rest in a way which allows them to take part in the Eucharist, refraining from work and activities which are incompatible with the sanctification of the Lord's day.

John Paul cited the Bible's creation story, canon law, and philosophers in his contemplative letter on the Sabbath.

Romanian Premier Radu Basile meets Tuesday with Pope John Paul

2

WEDNESDAY JULY 8 1998 www.news.com.au $1.

The Australian

The Pope last night issued a strongly worded appeal to restore the sacred nature of Sunday. **Michelle Gunn** reports on the social forces preying on the day of rest

THE SABBATH, REMEMBER?

JAMES MURRAY

Of course, the integrity of the family, a linchpin in the Pope's social campaign, relies upon the family being together at least some time. What better than a day instituted to be free from work?

The three main religions all have such days: Jews the Saturday Shabbat, Muslims the Friday prayers and Christians the Sunday. But it is the Jewish tradition which gives the sabbath divine authority. It derives from the Bible revelation that "God rested on the sabbath day, and made it holy".

"Certainly, Christians, by making Sunday the commemoration of Christ's resurrection, laid claim to a new sort of sabbath. Nevertheless, many became as absolute about their day of rest as the Jews, and were dubbed "Sabbatarians". They can be expected to cheer the Pope's letter!

There seems little doubt, too, that the Pope, so sensitive to Judaism, and well-versed in its traditions, appreciates the effect of the Jewish sabbath and the cohesiveness of the Jewish family.

Nevertheless, Hughes and others believe *Dies Domini* will strike a chord with people around the world, including worshippers from other denominations.

Is this really happening? Won't it just go away? Are there less than 500 days until the year 2000? So what? Will a smiling priest, as we see above, soon welcome some of us to our new home in the dungeon?

"Only those who have been diligent students of the Scriptures and who have received the love of the truth will be shielded from the powerful delusion that takes the world captive. By the Bible testimony these will detect the deceiver in his disguise. To all the testing time will come. By the sifting of temptation the genuine Christian will be revealed. Are the people of God now so firmly established upon His word that they would not yield to the evidence of their senses? Would they, in such a crisis, cling to the Bible and the Bible only? Satan will, if possible, prevent them

33:16. But many of all nations and of all classes, high and low, rich and poor, black and white, will be cast into the most unjust and cruel bondage. The beloved of God pass weary days, bound in chains, shut in by prison bars, sentenced to be slain, some apparently left to die of starvation in dark and loathsome dungeons. No human ear is open to hear their moans; no human hand is ready to lend them help.

"Will the Lord forget His people in this trying hour? Did He forget faithful Noah when judgments were visited upon

■ CONVERSATION

Plotting world order in Rome

Vatican expert Malachi Martin *tries to scope out papal succession*

Your novel depicts an international plot by Vatican insiders and internationalists to install a new pope and establish a "new world order." How fictional is this story line?

Not very. There is an unspoken alliance today between powers inside the Vatican and leaders of major international humanist organizations who would change the Roman Catholic Church from a sacred institution to one whose primary function is to act as a stabilizing social force in the world. They see the church as the only global structure able to do this. The one obstacle is John Paul II. He is seen as a defender of medieval traditions. They want a pope who shares their more liberal, globalist view.

Martin. *Unholy alliance?*

Who are these powers?

Cardinals of the church, the men who will elect the next pope. I describe them as conciliarists. The church today is divided. Monolithic faith is gone. The new rival factions: traditionalists who prefer the church as it was before the reforms of the Second Vatican Council and conciliarists who want to liberalize church doctrine on everything from divorce and contraception to abortion and homosexuality. The numbers are about even, but conciliarists hold the positions of power. They think John Paul II is too conservative; traditionalists don't think he is conservative enough.

What about the nonchurch part of the alliance? Who are they?

Academia, foundations, nongovernmental organizations, even some governmental agencies. They have vast resources devoted to population control, education and economic and social stabilization. If they can get the Roman Catholic Church to side with them in the social and cultural field in a world that is dysfunctional, they'll have another element of stability.

This sounds rather conspiratorial.

It's not a conspiracy, but it's deliberate. Conciliarists and nonchurch globalists think the same way. Neither likes the pope's policies. They are preparing for the selection of the next pope.

Why write this as fiction? Why not name names?

Some of the cardinals involved are well respected and loved. Understandably, many people would react emotionally in defense of the cardinals and would miss the larger point. I plan to write a monograph in the fall that names some names. ■

CONVERSATION WITH JEFFERY L. SHELER

Windswept House: A Vatican Novel, Doubleday, is published in June

U.S. News & World Report, June 10, 1996

that could properly ... dressed.

The Australian 6/10/93 Front page.

Vatican reasserts authority over conscience

from Peter Smith.

By ERROL SIMPER

THE first Vatican encyclical specifically framed for Catholic bishops and church teachers reasserts church authority over the individual conscience and is underpinned by a strong warning that the church's fundamental Christian message is "being distorted or denied" by dissenters.

The document says the conscience can err unless directed by divine wisdom, that morality cannot be a matter for democratic debate, and it directs bishops to adhere steadfastly to traditional church doctrine, however fierce the criticism that might attract.

Pope John Paul II's 179-page doctrinal text, released yesterday and unlikely to find too much favour with so-called church progressives, asks those responsible for handing down the faith to turn from theological questioning of church tenets, from attempting to adapt them to prevailing culture, and to continue to be unequivocal about "intrinsically evil acts" such as contraception.

The encyclical – Veritatis Splendor, or The Splendour of the Truth – concedes the Catholic Church is frequently accused of "intolerable intransigence" over moral questions, but says genuine love and compassion cannot flow from "ethical relativism" or from "compromising and falsifying the standard of good and evil".

The Pope, in the 15th year of his reign, does not specifically refer to increased pressure on the church to allow women priests or to modify its stance on abortion, but reinforces contraception as evil.

He rejects many modern concepts of individual freedoms – often advanced as allowing theological leeway for the church to accept female ordination and allow priests to marry.

He says the so-called freedom of the individual has been elevated to too high a plane and that individual conscience can be mistaken.

He goes on: "As the Apos Paul says, the conscie must be confirmed by T Holy Spirit. It must be cl it must not practise cunn and tamper with God's w but openly state the trut

The document rej what it calls "relativi pragmatism and posi ism", says moral theologi must exercise careful cernment "in the contex today's prevalently sc tific and technical cultu and says some values worth dying for.

Continued — Page 20

Morris West — Page 1

Two-page special report — Pages 19, 20

'Investment Business Daily

"For People who choose To Succeed"

Circulation 258,000 | Thursday, July 16, 1998 | Los Angeles, California

NATIONAL ISSUE: One Court For All The World?

By Brian Mitchell

'Rights' Tribunal Might Trample

Critics call it a blatant giveaway of American freedoms. Supporters say it's the only way to bring the world's worst murderers to justice.

A United Nations meeting in Rome is wrapping up five weeks of work on a proposed international criminal court. The new court would have worldwide jurisdiction and could investigate, indict, hold, try, and punish, those who committed certain crimes.

The Clinton Administration has long supported the idea in principle, but also sought veto power for members of the U N security Council over the court's investigations.

But observers now say U.S. negotiations in Rome may support a compromise put forth by Singapore. It would allow a majority vote in the Security Council to delay a court investigation, but not stop it.

The proposed international court would subject Americans to a new world authority, critics warn. Although the new court would have no police itself, it might use U.N. or other forces to nab suspects, even Americans.

"We're talking about creating here something that exercises genuine power, real put-people-in-jail power, but that is responsible to no one but itself," said Lee Casey, a constitutional lawyer with the Washington firm of Hunton & Williams.

It basically means that our leadership, the elected representatives of the American people, suddenly are not wholly accountable to the people, but to the court.

The Italian government even put up a billboard in Rome telling convention delegates, "We expect results."

Supporters of the international court deny that American rights will be infringed.

But critics fear political influence and abuses.

Meanwhile, the Clinton administration has accepted a provision in the International Criminal Court convention that permits it to step in when a country's legal system collapses or a nation has shown "extreme bad faith."

Oh friend, do you comprehend this Roman Catholic inspired horror? Surely what the prophet of God said about Rom regaining control of the world {GC 565}, and being about to spring her trap {GC 581} is true.

People of the U.S., and the other nations don't understand, but we who know the prophecies of God can see behind th scenes, and know what is quickly approaching.

"As Satan influenced Esau to march against Jacob, so he will stir up the wicked to destroy God's people. . .

"They afflict their souls before God, pointing to their past repentance of their many sins, and pleading the Saviour promise: 'Let him take hold of My strength, that he may make peace with Me; and he shall make peace with Me.' Isaia 27:5. Their faith does not fail because their prayers are not immediately answered. Though suffering the keenest anxiet terror, and distress, they do not cease their intercessions. They lay hold of the strength of God as Jacob laid hold of th Angel; and the language of their souls is: 'I will not let Thee go, except Thou bless me.'

"On every hand they hear the plottings of treason and see the active working of rebellion; and there is aroused with them an intense desire, an earnest yearning of soul, that this great apostasy may be terminated and the wickedness of tl wicked may come to an end. . .

torture us in basements of Catholic churches, bring us before courts with T.V. cameras, and sentence us to death? How long will that take?

"Christians today must face the enticements of a culture that has accepted the benefits of rest and free time, but that often uses them frivolously."

POPE JOHN PAUL II
In his letter, entitled "Dies Domini (The Day of the Lord)"

Atlanta Journal Constitution, July 8, 1998.

Group rejoices at pope's plea to keep Sabbath

By Jeffry Scott
STAFF WRITER

For 110 years it's been crusading — with Sundays off, of course.

And on Tuesday, the Atlanta-based Lord's Day Alliance of the United States got a helping hand from the pope in its long-running campaign to keep the faithful in their pews and out of the shopping malls on Sunday.

The pope's decree comes at a time when attendance at Sunday Mass has declined. That decline is a distressingly familiar issue to Jack Lowndes, executive director of the interdenominational Lord's Day Alliance.

"This is something we've been fighting a long time," Lowndes said Tuesday, wearing a blue seersucker suit and propped back in his office chair at the group's headquarters in the Baptist Center on the Mercer University campus. "If our founders were worried about people not resting on Sunday in 1888, I can't imagine what they'd think of things now.

"We believe what the Bible says: 'Remember the Sabbath and keep it holy.' It should be a day of rest, worship and good works."

Directors of a national pizza chain recently called to investigate how much business they'd lose if they closed on Sundays. The biggest grocery chain in Richmond, Ukrops, is closed on Sundays. So is Chick-fil-A, whose founder, S. Truett Cathy, is a member of the alliance's board.

And on Monday, the NCAA revealed that 99 universities have protested a rule that requires teams to play Sunday games.

"There is a growing movement to make Sunday a day of rest," Lowndes said. "And it's not all based on rest and worship, although that is why we support it."

Life is too frantic these days, he says. Americans need to kick back and relax.

5 JULY 1998 · THE SUNDAY TIMES

1·20 **WORLD NEWS**

Pope launches crusade to save Sunday

THE Pope will issue a strongly worded appeal to Roman Catholics this week to restore the sacred nature of Sunday. Prompted by concern that the sabbath has been undermined by business and falling attendances at mass in the West, he will urge Catholics to defend it as a day of worship and recreation for families.

Final preparations are being made at the Vatican to distribute an apostolic letter — or exhortation — on the subject from John Paul II. The document, Dies Domini (The Day of the Lord), is expected to be addressed to all "faithful Catholics" rather than only to bishops and priests.

Timed to coincide with the start of the summer holidays, when many people re-evaluate their lives away from the pressures of work, the exhortation is likely to form the subject of sermons over the next ... weeks.

It is also expected to win support from other churches — particularly from evangelical Christians — who share the Pope's anxiety about the erosion of the sabbath.

In Britain, Sunday opening at a growing number of shops has forced many people to work, making a traditional family day impossible. While the trend is less marked in other large European countries, including France, Germany and Italy, church-going has nevertheless been in decline.

Vatican sources say the Pope has resolved to emphasise the physical and practical benefits of a day of rest. One said he was keenly aware that a day off had become "a rare luxury" in some developing countries.

The exhortation is understood to be divided into three sections, considering the sabbath from the biblical point of view, assessing the extent of its erosion and setting out a way forward.

It will reflect an appeal made at the height of a debate about

by Christopher Morgan
Rome

Sunday opening in Rome four years ago, when the Pope warned Italians to remember the meaning of the day. In Vienna last month, he told Catholics: "Do whatever you can to preserve Sunday. Make it clear that this day must not be worked, since it must be celebrated as the day of our Lord."

The initiative is the latest in a

The Pope: strong appeal

"Make it clear that Sunday must not be worked, since it must be celebrated as the day of our Lord"

series on social issues by the 78-year-old pontiff, who, despite his evident frailty and the onset of Parkinson's disease, has left aides in no doubt about his determination to continue providing vigorous leadership into the new millennium.

Two of his most recent visits overseas — to Cuba and Nigeria — have been taken up largely with human rights questions. In another apostolic letter last week, he dismayed liberal Catholics by proposing to excommunicate those who persistently undermined orthodox teaching on a range of issues, including women priests, saying the church could not alter a "choice made by Christ" that only men should be ordained.

The Pope's exhortation on the sabbath, however, is intended to unite Catholics around the idea that being fully human means having sufficient time for both work and leisure. He argues that the dignity of man depends on reasserting a degree of control over his destiny that has been threatened by longer working hours and their encroachment on the sabbath.

Terence Phipps, a lecturer at the Allen Hall Seminary in London, said the notion of one day's rest came from the bib- ... of the creation in the Old Testament and was reasserted in the Ten Commandments. "The Lord's command is first and foremost to rest," he said. "Because people are free, the most natural thing to do is to worship and praise God on that day of rest."

In a sign of the broad Christian support the Pope can expect to command on the issue, David Phillips, director of the Church Society — an influential grouping within the Church of England — praised the initiative this weekend. "Anything the Pope says in line with the Bible is to be welcomed," Phillips said. "In this country, Sunday has fallen by the wayside and Christians need to recover its sacred character."

Gary Lysaght, a moral theologian at St John's Seminary in Wonersh, Surrey, also welcomed the forthcoming papal letter.

"It is good to be challenged about the importance of this day," he said. "Sadly in Britain B&Q and Sainsbury's seem to be the new churches and cathedrals."

can manipulate the minds of the people so that the Pope can openly demand the keeping of Sunday holy? Are we so close now to the end of the world that the Pope's call for worship will be welcomed? How long will that take?

The Detroit News

Tuesday, July 7, 1998 State Edition

Pope's call for worship welcomed

He warns Catholics to dedicate Sundays to celebrating God — not their free time.

By Mark Puls
and Charles Hurt
The Detroit News

Maryann Schreiber, a devout Catholic, works the late, late shift Saturday night and Sunday morning at a hotel.

She has to make a living, but the Hamtramck woman does so at the cost of mounting guilt over missing church Sunday mornings.

"I want to go back to the old ways where Sunday was the Lord's day," Schreiber said. "I agree with the pope. I want that life again."

In a day when computer modems are never fast enough and no one seems to have enough time for a full night's rest, Pope John Paul II is issuing a stern warning to Catholics that they should set aside Sunday for worship — not errands or their free time.

"This really is an extraordinary move," said Jay McNally, executive director of Call to Holiness, a Metro Detroit lay group that promotes traditional Catholic teachings. "This appears to be the strongest words the pope has issued. Period."

The pontiff used his weekly address Sunday from his window over St. Peter's Square to urge church members to make time to keep the Sabbath holy. And today, the Vatican is expected to issue an Apostolic letter from the pope further stressing the Third Commandment. Apostolic letters are incorporated into church rules.

Sundays have come to be "felt and lived only as a weekend," John Paul lamented Sunday. "It (should be) the weekly day in which the church celebrates the resurrection of Christ. In obedience to the Third Commandment, Sunday must be sanctified, above all, by participation in Holy Mass."

In his letter, the pope goes on to say a violator should be "punished as a heretic," said McNally, who read an unofficial English translation of the letter on a Vatican Web site.

Please see SUNDAYS, Page 2A

Associated Press

Pope John Paul II reminds Catholics that Sunday is a day of worship.

The Detroit News CyberSurvey

What do you think?

Pope John Paul II reminded Catholics of the sanctity of Sundays, saying that for many, the sabbath was "felt and lived only as a weekend." Do you spend Sunday as a day of worship, or a day of errands? Share your thoughts in Detroit News Online's CyberSurvey at http://detnews.com/current/metro/

Pivo

Famines will increase. Pestilences will sweep away thousands. Dangers are all around us from the powers without and satanic workings within, but the restraining power of God is now being exercised.--19MR 382.

"The plagues of God are already falling upon the earth, sweeping away the most costly structures as if by a breath of fire from heaven. Will not these judgments bring professing Christians to their senses?" 3MR 311 (1902).

"In the closing scenes of this earth's history many of these children and youth will astonish people by their witness to the truth, which will be borne in simplicity, yet with spirit and power. They have been taught the fear of the Lord, and t' hearts have been softened by a careful and prayerful study of the Bible. In the near future many children will be enuued with the Spirit of God and will do a work in proclaiming the truth to the world that at that time cannot well be done by the older members of the church." AH 489. Praise God!

The great God of heaven is going to finish His work in the earth and the devil and all his forces can't stop it! Our mighty God is in control. The devil's brain is like a string bean compared to the almighty power of King Jesus. But don't fool yourself. He hasn't finished doing his thing yet. Our kind Father is going to let him do to us what the monks of the inquisition did to many of His humble people. Why allow such a terrible thing? To save even more souls. That's what dear Jesus is interested in! By the grace of God, that's what I'm living for. How about you!

The devil's girlfriend Rome is on the march. She is attacking God's SDA church. I've said it a hundred times and I'll say it again - as an ordained SDA minister, **I'm standing in loyal defense of God's 600u year old SDA church against the horrible Roman Catholic attack going on against it.** Yes, an inquisition will happen again. It's just months away - the number of which only God knows. It will come into full bloom when the devil's Sunday law is passed. You already have evidence on the preceding pages that we are on the brink of it right now. When it comes, most Sabbath-keepers will cave in like they did when the Ustachis and Nazis threatened them with death. The time ahead of us will be very similar. Has God given us a hint of what it will be like? Has He revealed to us what will happen when even most church members cave in and go along with the soon-coming Sunday law - like in the dark ages - like with the Nazis, and Ustachi of WWII - like in the brainwashing of the communist prison camps of the Korean War? Watch closely.

"That night I dreamed that I was in Battle Creek looking out from the side glass at the door and saw a company marching up to the house, two and two. They looked stern and determined. I knew them well and turned to open the parlor door to receive them, but thought I would look again. The scene was changed. The company now presented the appearance of a Catholic procession. One bore in his hand a cross, another a reed. And as they approached, the one carrying a reed made a circle around the house, saying three times: 'This house is proscribed. The goods must be co''scated. They have spoken against our holy order.' Terror seized me, and I ran through the house, out of the north d..., and found myself in the midst of a company, some of whom I knew, but I dared not speak a word to them for fear of being betrayed. I tried to seek a retired spot where I might weep and pray without meeting eager, inquisitive eyes wherever I turned. I repeated frequently: 'If I could only understand this! If they will tell me what I have said or what I have done!'

"I wept and prayed much as I saw our goods confiscated. I tried to read sympathy or pity for me in the looks of those around me, and marked the countenances of several whom I thought would speak to me and comfort me if they did not fear that they would be observed by others. I made one attempt to escape from the crowd, but seeing that I was watched, I concealed my intentions. I commenced weeping aloud, and saying: 'If they would only tell me what I have done or what I have said!' My husband, who was sleeping in a bed in the same room, heard me weeping aloud and awoke me. My pillow was wet with tears." 1T 578.

Will we soon see headlines and articles pushing for the devil's Sunday law? How long will that take?

opinion

St. Petersburg Times

Restore Sunday as a day of rest, reader urges

letters

Today it is a shame: A child doesn't even know the difference between a weekday, Sunday or a holiday. It's work, work, work, or shop, shop, shop. How much can one shop?

It's this terrible greed that is pushing these businesses to remain open such long hours and on almost every holiday. Why not try to put a stop to it? We, the public, are the only ones who can.

Why not send a petition through your neighborhood? I'm sure you will get plenty of signatures. You can then send copies to your representatives in Tallahassee and Washington and see if we can get a Blue Law passed. Then maybe we can all get to know the meaning of a Sunday and a holiday again.

Why not take a lesson from all our government agencies? Nobody works on Saturday or Sunday, not even the president. Let us wake up before we destroy ourselves with this greed.

Mary Johnson
Port Richey

DATELINE: SUNDAY LAW

THE NATIONAL SUNDAY LAW IS COMING! IS IT CONSTITUTIONAL? IS IT BIBLICAL?

Vatican Admits Sunday is NOT the Biblical Sabbath

In a recent Catholic church newsletter, it stated, "Perhaps the boldest thing, the most revolutionary change the Church ever did, happened in the first century [actually it happened in the fourth century]. The holy day, the Sabbath, was changed from Saturday to Sunday. 'The Day of the Lord' [Dies Domini] was chosen, not from any direction noted in the Scriptures, but from the Church's sense of its own power.... People who think that the Scriptures should be the sole authority, should logically become [Seventh-day] Adventists, and keep Saturday holy." *Saint Catherine Catholic Church Sentinel*, Algonac, Michigan, May 21, 1995.

No Scriptural Support

"Sunday is a Catholic institution and its claim to observance can be defended only on Catholic principles.... From beginning to end of Scripture there is not a single passage that warrants the transfer of weekly public worship from the last day of the week to the first."—*Catholic Press*, Sydney, Australia, August, 1900.

The Vatican's Mark of Authority

"Sunday is our mark of authority.... The church is above the Bible, and this transference of sabbath observance is proof of that fact." *The Catholic Record*, London, Ontario, September 1, 1923.

Catholic Catechism

"Question: Which is the Sabbath day?"

"Answer: Saturday is the Sabbath."

"Question: Why do we observe Sunday instead of Saturday?"

"Answer: We observe Sunday instead of Saturday because the Catholic Church in the Council of Laodicea (A.D. 336) transferred the solemnity from Saturday to Sunday." *The Convert's Catechism of Catholic Doctrine*, by Peter Geiermann, 50.

IMPORTANT INFORMATION

What will happen to our nation if we force people to worship on Sunday? This #1 bestseller, *The Great Controversy*, addresses this important question, and much more.

Order today, call 1-800-774-3566

- The news media can tell you what's happening. This book will tell you what *will happen* and *why*.
- 426 pages, PB, $10.95 Postage included!
- You may read this book in various languages and download it by visiting our website at:

www.sundaylaw.org

' 19, 1998 ANALYSIS OUR SUNDAY VISITOR 3

'he Holy Father lays down the doctrinal law

›pe John Paul II spells out the Church's teaching authority, obligations of the faithful in *Ad Tuendam Fidem*

BY JOHN NORTON

[VATICAN CITY]

he face of an "impelling necessity to vent and confute the opinions of the-gians which have arisen against" a cer-ı category of Church teachings, Pope n Paul II has underlined that being :holic involves believing what the urch teaches.

Vhoever "obstinately" denies these ths, the doctrinal commentary says, ; under the censure of heresy.

> This is "clearly a development of the dogma of infallibility."

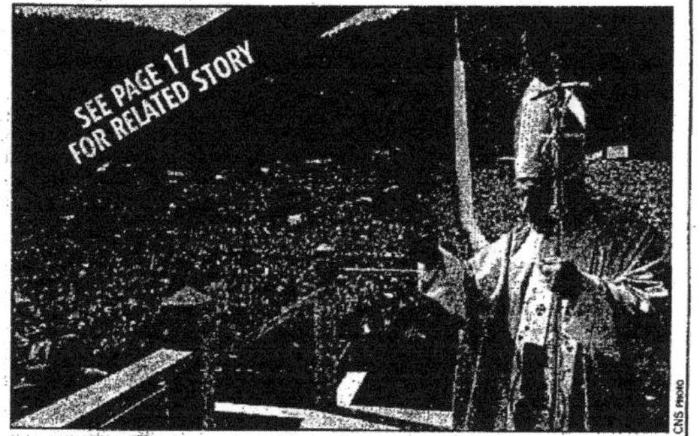

TELLING IT LIKE IT IS: Pope John Paul II

THE TIMES MONDAY JULY 6 1998

WORLD IN BRIEF

Pope urges flock to keep Sunday sacred

Rome: The Pope yesterday urged Christians to rediscover the value of Sunday, even if it meant going against the grain of a society that sees it as just part of the weekend. He also urged Roman Catholics to use their holidays to restore the spirit as well as the body.

Giving his last Sunday message in St Peter's Square until after the summer, he spoke of the theme of a new Apostolic Letter, *Dies Domini* (The Day of the Lord), that he will issue tomorrow. The Pope said Sundays should be treated as sacred.

"Today, to remain faithful [to the tradition of Sunday] one very often has swim upstream," he said. The new document is expected to address issues such as Sunday business and dedicating the day to the family. *(Reuters)*

DAILY MAIL - 6/7/98

Pope's plea for sacred Sunday

POPE John Paul II yesterday urged Christians to keep Sunday as a holy day. He said the true value of the sabbath must be rediscovered, even if it meant going against the grain of a society which sees it as just a part of the weekend. 'Sunday is something much different, it is the weekly day in which the church celebrates the resurrection of Christ,' he said. 'In obedience to the Third Commandment, Sunday must be sanctified, above all by participation in holy Mass.' The 78-year-old pontiff looked tired as he spoke in St Peter's Square for the last time before his long summer break. Tomorrow the Vatican is to issue the his latest Apostolic Letter, 'Dies Domini' (The Day of the Lord), in which he is expected to address the themes of commercial activities on Sundays and dedicating the day to the family.

Chicago SUNDAY STAR

Does your family matter to you?

We think so.

We believe that the majority support Sunday as a Day of Rest.

What is The Lord's Day Alliance of the United States?

We insist that merchants close their places of business on Sunday.

We commend those who close on Sunday and those who refust to shop on Sunday.

We pray for proper observance of the Lord's Day for our nation and for ask prayers for The Lord's Day Alliance of the United States.

We suggest that letters be written to editors, legislators, mayors, governors, congressmen and the President of the United States and that we speak to our representatives in government about using their influence for passing Sabbath laws that are constitutional.

We suggest that we write union and industrial leaders.

We write retail merchant's associations and urge them to get together and demand that businesses stay closed on Sunday.

We write owners and confer with managers of businesses and owners and managers of malls.

We get the message on radio and television wherever possible.

We encourage churches, denominations, and organizations to pass appropriate resolutions.

DR. JAMES P. WESBERRY
Executive Director
The Lord's Day Alliance of the United States
Suite 107 / 2930 Flowers Road, South
Atlanta, GA 30341

Cape Cod Times of Hyannis.

YOU ARE CORDIALLY INVITED TO ATTEND AN ECUMENICAL RALLY FOR THE PURPOSE OF KEEPING SUNDAY AS A DAY OF REST FOR THE WORKING CITIZENS OF OUR NATION AND FOR OUR BLOOD BOUGHT LIBERTY TO WORSHIP GOD ON THAT DAY OF THE WEEK

Guest Speakers are as follows:

Rev. James P. Wesberry
Distinguished Baptist Minister
of Atlanta, Georgia
Rev. Roger V. Kvam, pastor
First Presbyterian Church
Quincy, Massachusetts

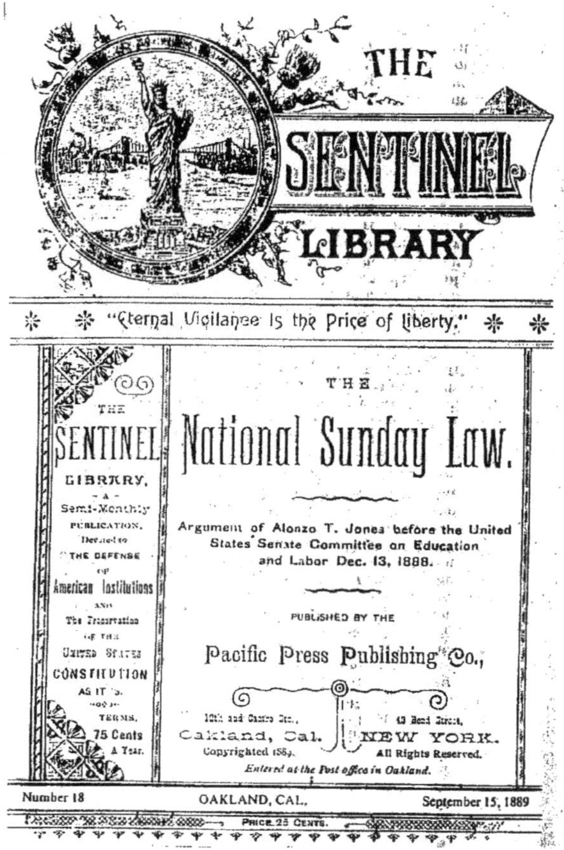
THE
SENTINEL
LIBRARY
"Eternal Vigilance Is the Price of Liberty."
THE
SENTINEL
LIBRARY,
A
Semi-Monthly
PUBLICATION,
Devoted to
THE DEFENSE
OF
American Institutions
AND
The Preservation
OF THE
UNITED STATES
CONSTITUTION
AS IT IS.
TERMS,
75 Cents
A Year.
THE
National Sunday Law.
Argument of Alonzo T. Jones before the United States Senate Committee on Education and Labor Dec. 13, 1888.
PUBLISHED BY THE
Pacific Press Publishing Co.,
12th and Castro Sts., Oakland, Cal.
43 Bond Street, NEW YORK.
Copyrighted 1889.
All Rights Reserved.
Entered at the Post-office in Oakland.
Number 18
OAKLAND, CAL.,
September 15, 1889
PRICE 25 CENTS.

The bill proposed by Senator Blair, and upon which the argument was made, is as follows: —

"50th CONGRESS, } S. 2983.
1st SESSION. }

"IN the Senate of the United States, May 21, 1888, Mr. Blair introduced the following bill, which was read twice, and referred to the Committee on Education and Labor: —

"A bill to secure to the people the enjoyment of the first day of the week, commonly known as the Lord's day, as a day of rest, and to promote its observance as a day of religious worship.

"*Be it enacted by the Senate and House of Representatives of the United States of America in Congress assembled*, That no person, or corporation, or the agent, servant, or employee of any person or corporation, shall perform or authorize to be performed any secular work, labor, or business to the disturbance of others, works of necessity, mercy, and humanity excepted; nor shall any person engage in any play, game, or amusement, or recreation, to the disturbance of others, on the first day of the week, commonly known as the Lord's day, or during any part thereof, in any territory, district, vessel, or place subject to the exclusive jurisdiction of the United States; nor shall it be lawful for any person or corporation to receive pay for labor or service performed or rendered in violation of this section.

"SEC. 2. That no mails or mail matter shall hereafter be transported in time of peace over any land postal route, nor shall any mail matter be collected, assorted, handled, or delivered during any part of the first day of the week: *Provided*, That whenever any letter shall relate to a work of necessity or mercy, or shall concern the health, life, or decease of any person, and the fact shall be plainly stated upon the face of the envelope containing the same, the postmaster-general shall provide for the transportation of such letter.

"SEC. 3. That the prosecution of commerce between the States and with the Indian tribes, the same not being work of necessity, mercy, or humanity, by the transportation of persons or property by land or water in such way as to interfere with or disturb the people in the enjoyment of the first day of the week, or any portion thereof, as a day of rest from labor, the same not being labor of necessity, mercy, or humanity, or its observance as a day of religious worship, is hereby prohibited; and any person or corporation, or the agent or employee of any person or corporation, who shall willfully violate this section, shall be punished by a fine of not less than ten nor more than one thousand dollars, and no service performed in the prosecution of such prohibited commerce shall be lawful, nor shall any compensation be recoverable or be paid for the same.

"SEC. 4. That all military and naval drills, musters, and parades, not in time of active service or immediate preparation therefor, of soldiers, sailors, marines, or cadets of the United States, on the first day of the week, except assemblies for the due and orderly observance of religious worship, are hereby prohibited, nor shall any unnecessary labor be performed or permitted in the military or naval service of the United States on the Lord's day.

"SEC. 5. That it shall be unlawful to pay or to receive payment or wages in any manner for service rendered, or for labor performed, or for the transportation of persons or of property in violation of the provisions of this act, nor shall any action lie for the recovery thereof, and when so paid, whether in advance or otherwise, the same may be recovered back by whoever shall first sue for the same.

"SEC. 6. That labor or service performed and rendered on the first day of the week in consequence of accident, disaster, or unavoidable delays in making the regular connections upon postal routes and routes of travel and transportation, the preservation of perishable and exposed property, and the regular and necessary transportation and delivery of articles of food in condition for healthy use, and such transportation for short distances from one State, district, or Territory,

into another State, district, or Territory as by local laws shall be declared to be necessary for the public good, shall not be deemed violations of this act, but the same shall be construed, so far as possible, to secure to the whole people rest from toil during the first day of the week, their mental and moral culture, and the religious observance of the Sabbath day."

Rev. A. H. Lewis, D. D., representative of the Seventh-day Baptists, had spoken, and asked that a section be added to the bill granting exemption to observers of the Seventh day; but in answering the questions that were asked by the Chairman, Mr. Lewis compromised his position, and was followed soon after by Dr. Herrick Johnson, of Chicago, who remarked that Dr. Lewis had "given his whole case away." This is what is referred to in my introductory remarks to the effect that we did not intend to "give *our* case away."

A. T. J.

Fort Worth Star-Telegram

WEDNESDAY, OCTOBER 27, 1993 — Fort Worth, Texas ★ Where The West Begins — 25¢ in Tarrant/Dallas counties 50¢ elsewhere

…on A, Page 10 / Fort Worth Star-Telegram / Wednesday, October 27, 1993

…oman Catholic leaders back U.S. role as world's police officer

BY DAVID BRIGGS
The Associated Press

…e United States should keep its …on nuclear testing, stop ped…g its arms around the world, and …its swords into plowshares in …ral America, Africa and the …dle East, the nation's Roman …olic leaders say.

…e proposal calling for the Unit…ates to combat a groundswell of …tionism comes a decade after …ishops' pastoral letter on nucle…ms propelled them into U.S. public policy debates at the height of the Cold War.

The new statement, "The Harvest of Justice is Sown in Peace," says that the United States retains a moral responsibility to intervene — with force if necessary — in regional conflicts and to increase humanitarian aid to countries where it once battled communism.

The statement was written by some of the nation's most influential bishops, including Cardinals Joseph Bernardin of Chicago and Roger Mahony of Los Angeles; Archbishop John R. Roach of Minneapolis, chairman of the bishops' International Policy Committee; and Bishop James Malone of Youngstown, Ohio, a former president of the National Conference of Catholic Bishops.

Gen. Colin Powell, former chairman of the Joint Chiefs of Staff, was among those to appear before the committee.

The committee will present the policy statement to the full conference at its meeting Nov. 15-18 in Washington.

A decade ago, the bishops' pastoral letter "The Challenge of Peace" drew a firestorm of protest from critics inside the church and in the Reagan administration for its calls to reduce military spending and the nation's nuclear arsenal.

Critics said the bishops should stick to advising its 58 million-member flock on ecclesiastical matters. But the public attention that greeted the bishops' foray into U.S. military policy proved a watershed event in propelling religious bodies into the forefront of public policy debates.

The bishops said the challenge for peace today is different than at the end of the Cold War, but no less urgent.

"After the Cold War, there has emerged an understandable but dangerous temptation to turn inward, to focus only on domestic needs and to ignore global responsibilities. This is not an option for believers in a universal church or for citizens in the world's most powerful nation," the bishops said.

In the new statement, perhaps the first comprehensive religious blueprint for U.S. military policy after the Cold War, the bishops resist calls for unilateral disarmament but say nuclear deterrence is morally acceptable only if it is a step toward progressive disarmament.

Charleston, S.C.

GC 444, 445, 616, 588
7BC 975
ST 451

4-A—The Post and Courier, Wednesday, March 30, 1994

Evangelicals join Catholics in unity bid

Associated Press

NEW YORK — They toiled together in the vineyards of the movements against abortion and pornography, and now leading Catholics and evangelicals are asking their flocks for a remarkable leap of faith: to finally accept each other as Christians.

In what's being called a historic declaration, evangelicals including Pat Robertson and Charles Colson joined with conservative Roman Catholic leaders Tuesday in upholding the ties of faith that bind the nation's largest and most politically active religious groups.

They urged Catholics and evangelicals to increase their efforts against abortion and pornography and to lobby for value-laden education, but to no longer hold each other at theological arm's length and to stop aggressive proselytization of each other's flocks.

"As evangelicals and Catholics, we dare not by needless and loveless conflict between ourselves give aid and comfort to the enemies of the cause of Christ," said the signers of "Evangelicals and Catholics Together: The Christian Mission in the Third Millennium."

John White, president of Geneva College and former president of the National Association of Evangelicals, said the statement represents a "triumphalistic moment" in American religious life after centuries of distrust.

"I really do think it is a historic moment. I don't know of any other time in history when these two communities have stood together, spoken together" on matters of faith, White said.

The consultation was started in 1992 by Colson, the former Watergate figure who founded the international Prison Fellowship ministry, and the Rev. Richard Neuhaus, director of the Institute on Religion and Public Life in New York. The document, which does not represent an official stance of any denomination, was drafted during the next two years by a group of evangelical and Catholic scholars. Forty people had signed the document by Tuesday.

On the Catholic side, endorsers include Archbishop Francis Stafford of Denver, Bishop Carlos A. Sevilla of the Archdiocese of San Francisco and prominent theologians such as Neuhaus and Michael Novak, recent winner of the Templeton Prize for Progress in Religion.

Other evangelical endorsers include the heads of the Home Mission Board and Christian Life Commission of the Southern Baptist Convention, the nation's largest Protestant denomination, and Bill Bright, founder of Campus Crusade for Christ.

In the last generation, it has become common for evangelicals and Catholics to work together on issues such as abortion, pornography, vouchers for religious education and voluntary school prayer. But evangelical leaders often placated their most conservative members with the assurance the alliance was only for practical ends.

What's different in the statement is the effort to turn the theological swords honed over centuries of conflict into a recognition of the common faith.

"We together, evangelicals and Catholics, confess our sins against the unity that Christ intends for all his disciples," the statement says.

GC 573
7T 182
RH 6-1-1886, p. 338

...ristian Science Monitor, Monday, May 4, 1998.

On the Seventh Day – They Closed Shop

ST. LOUIS

They come from different walks of life and different faiths. They run businesses as diverse as fast-food restaurants and hardware rental stores. Yet they share a common conviction: Sundays are special.

So every seventh day these business people, across the country, pull down the window shade and quietly close up shop.

PHOTO BY DOUG ... SPECIAL TO THE CHRISTIAN SCIENCE MONITOR

SUNDAYS OFF: Bryan Swedlund and his family attend their St. Louis church weekly – thanks to his employer's no-Sunday policy.

Oh friend, the documentation you've just seen is only the tip end of a mountain a hundred miles high. The prophet of God cries out to us - - "Satan puts his interpretation upon events, and they think, as he would have them, that the calamities which fill the land are a result of Sundaybreaking. Thinking to appease the wrath of God these influential men make laws enforcing Sunday observance.--10MR 239.

"Protestants will throw their whole influence and strength on the side of the papacy. By a national act enforcing the false sabbath they will give life and vigor to the corrupt faith of Rome, reviving her tyranny and oppression of conscience." *Last Day Events*, p. 128.

"We have before us a great work--the closing work of centers of our work. Consider the amount of time, the

Vatican pushes for Sunday Legislation

In Europe the Sunday Law issue is expected to be contentions as Pope John Paul 2 continues to press for mandatory Sunday closing laws. (Church state May 1992.) Currently the Vatican is asking the civil authorities to cooperate with church in legislation of Sunday as the nation's day of rest. The civil authorities should be urged to cooperate with the church in maintaining and strengthening this public worship to god

And to support with our own authority the regulations set down by the church's pastors. For it is in this way that the faithful will understand why it is Sunday and not the Sabbath day that we are to keep holy. Roman Catechism 1986

What do you think?

If the civil authorities pass a nation Sunday law, does that prove that Sunday is the Sabbath day for man?

Should the civil authorizes pass a nation Sunday law because they are pleasured by religious powers?

Should individuals be penalized for worshiping on a different day other than Sunday?

Does it seem reasonable to you that the Church of Rome would push for Sunday legislation when they admit that Sunday is not the true biblical day of rest?

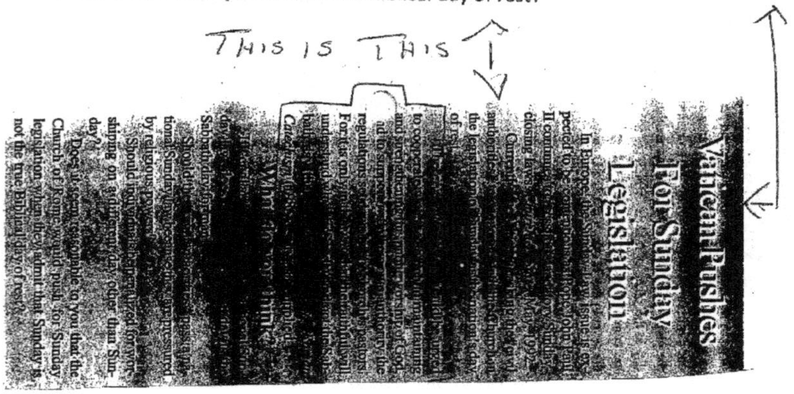

Never on Sunday

To allow employees more time
for family and worship,
this Hobby Lobby will be
CLOSED
SUNDAYS

5-7-98 Eric Schultz/Huntsville Times

Terri Thomas, assistant manager of the Hobby Lobby on South Memorial Parkway, places a sign on the ...nt of the store informing customers that the business will begin closing on Sundays starting May 10.

Some retailers closing for religious reasons

By RICK DAVIS
Times Business Writer

Those 33 Hobby Lobby stores are joining 15 others in the 162-store chain that are closing on Sundays.

After years of battling "blue laws," which prohibited certain kinds of businesses from opening on Sundays, a few other regional and national retailers are pulling back from seven-days-a-week operations. Chick-Fil-A founder Truett Cathy has always refused to open his chicken-sandwich restaurants on Sundays. And local restaurateur David Martin, who owns and operates Steak-Out locations and Rosie's Mexican Cantina, decided three years ago to close his stores on Sundays.

"When we first closed we had an initial drop in sales, but within six months we had caught our old sales levels and began having record weeks again."

— David Martin
Founder, Steak-Out

said. "But within six weeks, sales in those stores were actually running ahead of 1997 for the same period."

Alabama laws regarding businesses being open on Sundays date back to 1852. Antebellum legislators fixed the penalty for any person "who engages in shooting, hunting, gaming, card playing or racing on that day, or who, being a merchant or shopkeeper, druggist excepted, keeps open store on Sunday," at a fine of no less than $10 and no more $100, and a jail sentence of no more than three months.

The term "blue law," depending

Business was good. But the ...rs were long. When one of ...tin's best store managers, Mary Ray, plopped down in a chair and said, "David Martin, y'all have been good to me. I make good money and I like my job, but I don't think I can go on much longer."

Martin's decision was based in the belief that his people — including himself and his wife, Rhonda — needed a day off. Religion was part of the decision, because "that was a day for most people's worship. Not all people worship that day. But for the majority, it would give them time for church and to be with their families."

Bill Hane says Hobby Lobby will remain closed on Sunday as long as possible. "We just feel like God honors people who do the right thing," Hane said. "There's an old saying that says, 'If your religion and business don't mix, there's something wrong with your business.'

You will see more and more of this type of thing in the comin

4 The Columbus Dispatch

Weary workers want day of rest

Christine Wicker
...as Morning News

Movement to reclaim Sabbath grows

DALLAS — Ken Nichols is suing to keep his Sunday.

The Fort Worth, Texas, car dealer's determination to stay closed on the Christian Sabbath is not about religion, said the owner of Nichols Ford in Fort Worth. It is not about business. It's about standing up to a money-mad, work-crazed world. It's about saying, "Enough."

Nichols' "enough" is being echoed — faintly — around the country by stressed-out, weary workers who need the break God intended them to have, said Jack Lowndes, whose job it is to listen for such reverberations.

The executive director of the Lord's Day Alliance of the United States can't really prove his contention.

"We've tried to do some tracking. I wouldn't say it's scientific ... but we're seeing more churches address the issue," said Lowndes, whose interdenominational group formed 110 years ago to protect the Christian Sabbath.

Tuesday, Pope John Paul II issued an apostolic letter that addresses respect for the Sabbath. In May, New York Cardinal John O'Connor created a national stir when he chastised soccer officials for scheduling children's games on Sunday mornings.

Determination to defend the day of rest is also coming from nonreligious quarters, said Jonathan Wilson, professor of religious studies at Westmont College in Santa Barbara, Calif.

"I think we are getting a little worn down as a people and as a culture and we're saying, 'Wouldn't it be nice if we all were off on this day?'" he said. "Part of it is nostalgia, but maybe we're also saying, 'There may be something emotionally and psychologically right about this idea of the Sabbath. Maybe God knew what he was doing.'"

"You can be successful and be closed on Sunday," he said.

system planned? How long will that take?

RICHMOND TIMES DISPATCH *MONDAY, JULY 20, 1998*

National ID system planned

...SHINGTON — As legislation that ...d protect patient privacy languishes in Congress, the Clinton administration is quietly laying plans to assign every American a "unique health identifier."

The ID would be a code that could be used to create a national database to track every citizen's medical history from cradle to grave.

The electronic code was mandated by a 1996 law and would be the first comprehensive national identification system since the Social Security number was introduced in 1935.

Although the idea has attracted almost no public attention, it is so contentious that federal health officials, who were supposed to propose a plan for the identifier by February, have made little headway. They are instead launching a series of hearings beginning today in Chicago to solicit public comment.

Proponents, including insurance companies and public health researchers, say the benefits would be vast. Doctors and hospitals would be able to monitor the health of patients as they switch from one insurance plan to the next. Patients would not have to wade through a cumbersome bureaucracy to obtain old records. Billing would be streamlined, saving money. A national disease database could be created, offering unlimited opportunities for scientific study.

But opponents, including privacy advocates and some doctors' groups, say the code smacks of Big Brother. They warn that sensitive health information might be linked to financial data or criminal records and that already tenuous privacy protections would be further weakened as existing managed-care databases, for example, are linked.

"We have very grave concerns about the unique patient identifier," said Dr. Donald Palmisano, the American Medical Association's expert on medical privacy. "If this information ended up in some central repository, some giant clearinghouse, what protection do we have that some vandal would not break in?"

The identifier was ordered by Congress in 1996 as part of legislation that permits employees to take their health insurance with them when they switch jobs. The Health Insurance Portability and Accountability Act also requires codes for employers, health plans, doctors and hospitals.

Experts say crucial questions remain, among them what kind of identifier should be used. Some have proposed using the Social Security number, which is already used as an identifier by many health plans. But critics complain that too many people, including credit-card company clerks, already have access to Social Security numbers.

Others have suggested a composite number, consisting of the patient's date of birth, the latitude and longitude of their hometown and some additional digits. Still others say the identifier should not be a number at all but rather a "biomedical marker," like a thumb print.

DECISIONS, PONDERINGS, THOUGHTS
What should I do?

In Acts 5:29, Luke wrote: *"Then Peter and the apostles answered and said, we ought to obey* ***God*** *rather than* ***men****."*

"Whether it be good, or whether it be evil, we will obey the voice of the LORD our God, to whom we send thee; that it may be well with us, when we obey the voice of the LORD our God" (Jeremiah 42:6).

Religions hear call of environment

ASSOCIATED PRESS

"The earth is the Lord's, and the fullness thereof," reads Psalm 24. People don't own this planet, in the biblical perspective, but are assigned by God as its caretakers.

That mandate and other biblical pointers to the singular value of the natural environment and humanity's responsibility of caring for it have aroused America's religious forces to that cause.

"It is what God made and beheld as good that is under assault" says a broad cross-section of religious leaders. "The future of this gift so freely given is in our hands, and we must maintain it as we have received it. . . . This is an inescapably religious challenge."

With observance of Earth Day this week and an ecumenical Ecology Sunday this weekend, churches are planning strong representation at the United Nations Earth Summit in Rio de Janeiro June 1-12, which involves governmental delegates and thousands of others from around the world.

An ecumenically backed Environmental Sabbath was set June 7 to call attention to the international efforts to safeguard nature.

Churches have "drawn together about this," says the Rev. Ken Grant of the Presbyterian Church (U.S.A.), based in Louisville, Ky. "We woke up. We've been sobered to learn of the harm being done to the environment."

Virtually every major religious body or their leaders, Protestant, Roman Catholic, Eastern Orthodox and Jewish, have joined the effort in the last few years, with a growing crescendo of concern.

"The web of life is one," U.S. Roman Catholic bishops said last November, adding that the task of sustaining human life itself "cannot be separated from the care and defense of all of creation."

Most major Protestant denominations, the Episcopal Church, United Methodist Church, American Baptist Churches and the United Church of Christ, among others, have adopted calls to safeguard nature.

Judaism plunged strongly into the movement in an unusually inclusive meeting in mid-March of leaders of all four wings of that faith, Orthodox, Conservative, Reform and Reconstructionist.

"For Jews, the environmental crisis is a religious challenge," the group said. "As heirs to a tradition of stewardship that goes back to Genesis and that teaches us to be partners in the ongoing work of Creation, we cannot accept the escalating destruction of our environment."

It "is our sacred duty as Jews to . . . take action."

DAN 3: 2,3,4,7,12,14 the words Setup is mention. Now the United Nations is using the same words setup. In Daniels day it was a golden image setup for the people to worship, today a law is being passed to worship on an Environmental Sunday Sabbath set on June 7, 1992.
If you refuse to worship on this day that is being setup by the United Nation or the world government you can not buy or sell.

www.ingramcontent.com/pod-product-compliance
Lightning Source LLC
Chambersburg PA
CBHW071542040426
42452CB00008B/1084
9781945975417